Beverly Hills
MANNERS

Beverly Hills
MANNERS

Golden Rules from the World's Most Glamorous Zip Code

Lisa Gaché

Skyhorse Publishing

Skyhorse Publishing books may be purchased in bulk at special discounts for sales promotion, corporate gifts, fund-raising, or educational purposes. Special editions can also be created to specifications. For details, contact the Special Sales Department, Skyhorse Publishing, 307 West 36th Street, 11th Floor, New York, NY 10018 or info@skyhorsepublishing.com.

Skyhorse® and Skyhorse Publishing® are registered trademarks of Skyhorse Publishing, Inc.®, a Delaware corporation.

www.skyhorsepublishing.com

10 9 8 7 6 5 4 3 2

Library of Congress Cataloging-in-Publication Data is available on file.

Print ISBN: 978-1-62914-585-3
Ebook ISBN: 978-1-62914-869-4

Printed in the United States of America

For my girls, Sydney and Dylan, who fuel my passion for manners, and for my husband, Brad, who embodies them naturally, every single day.

Contents

Welcome to Beverly Hills   1

Chapter 1: Keeping Up Appearances

No Second Chances:
   First Impressions, Lasting Impact   10
Fake It Until You Make It   11
Poise, Confidence, Acting Skills   11
Look the Part (or Someone Else Will Get It)   11
Wardrobe Malfunction!   13
Body Language Needs No Translation App   14
Slow Down the Beat   15
How to Land Safely into a Chair   16
Outtake: How to Walk in High Heels   17
Lights, Cameras, Close-ups, Oh My!   19
Clip It, Clean It, but Don't Cause Injury   20
Wipe Down All Exposed Surfaces   21
Keep Unsightly Habits Out of Sight   23
A Fashion Versus Style Smackdown   24
Outtake: A Few Tips About Apparel   26
First I look at the Purse   27
Outtake: Stash and Carry   28

Chapter 2: Pleased to Meet Me

If You Could Hear Yourself Talk . . .   30
Easy on the Ears   30
Language!   31
Meet and Greet, Neat   33
The Winning Handshake   35
Eye-to-Eye   37
Please Be Careful Not to Stare   37
Outtake: The Name Game   39
Outtake: Addressing the Ladies   40
Smack! Incoming Air Kiss   42

Chapter 3: Indirect Communications

A Word about Privacy   44
Telephony   45
Mind Your Mobile Manners   49
Texting and Subtexting   50
Old-Fashioned Email   52
Get It Right in Writing   54
Support the US Postal Service   54
Thank You for Writing a Thank-You Note   55
Unsocial Media   57
Tweet Me? Tweet You!   58
Killing Time on Facebook   60
Someone Is Watching You Read This Right Now 61

Chapter 4: Step Into My Office

You Got the Interview. Now What?   65
Separate Yourself from the Pack   66
Suit Up   67

Hug It Out or Just Shake Hands?   70
Age Before Beauty (There Is an Established
    Hierarchy)   71
Get Actual Business Cards   72
Leave It at Home: Personal Business at Work   73
Go Pro   74
There Will Be Meetings   77
Answer the Phone!   78
Everyone Looks Like Hell on Skype   79
Power Dinnering   80
Global Economy 101   83
Outtake: A Quick Trip Around the World
    of Business Protocols   85

Chapter 5: On Location

First of All, You'll Need a Date   89
Revive Chivalry   91
Outtake: Dating in the Digital Age   93
Now Make Your Grand Entrance   96
Outtake: Hit the Red Carpet
    Like a Rock Star   96
Superstar Service   99
Dine with Decorum   100
Outtake: The Tipping Point   107
Strict Diets Versus Annoyingly Picky Eaters   108
Taking Tea in Beverly Hills   110
Never Let 'Em See You Sweat   111
Expose Yourself to Art   115
Home Entertainment   117
The Invitation Sets the Tone   117
The Social Cost of Not RSVPing   118

Dinner Party Circuit 119
Outtake: Host a Marvelous Dinner Party 120
Outtake: Be a Fabulous Dinner Guest 122
Mutually Exclusive: A Day at the Country Club 123
High Social Anxiety 124
The Dreaded One-on-One 126
Outtake: Ice-breakers 127
Outtake: Conversation Killers 130

**Chapter 6: Stress-Free Holidays
(There's no such thing.)**

Shopping without Dropping 134
The Family Trap 135
The Holiday Gift Extravaganza 136
Rules of Re-gifting 139
Beware the Office Party 140

Chapter 7: Happy Houseguesting

Good Guest Check List 144
The Never-Coming-Back List of Things to Do 146

Chapter 8: The Cordial Bride

Family, Stress, Money: Who Pays for What? 148
Outtake: How Not to Ruin
Someone's Nuptials 149
The Overexposed Wedding 150
Bachelorette Party Debacles 151
Finally, the Big Day 153
Runaway Brides, Runaway Grooms,
and Broken Engagements 154

Chapter 9: Planes, Trains, Roads, and Rage

Bumper-to-Bumper Frustration   158
Brother, Can You Spare a Parking Space?   160
Civil Aviation   162
Elevator to the Stars   166

Chapter 10: Child Wrangling

Check Your Bags at the Door   171
Fun Is Your Best Teaching Partner   172
Don't Encase Your Kids in Lucite   175
Make the Dinner Table a Demilitarized Zone   178
Outtake: Personal Space with Siblings   180
Outtake: Chores for All Ages   180
Domestiquette   181
Socializing Children in the Pack   183
Techno-Babysitting   184
The Playdating Game   185
Hell Is Other People's Children   187
Outtake: Petiquette   188
This Is an Ad for Summer Camp   191
Outtake: Birthday Parties for Beginners   193
Children in Tow   195
Outtake: Air Travel with Offspring   198
The Holiday Marathon with Kids   198
The Bar/Bat Mitzvah Open Season   200
Entrance to Private School Is Destiny   202
You Made It in. Congrats!   208
Zero Tolerance: Cliques, Cattiness, and Bullying   213
Bad Sportsmanship   215
Back to School for Parents   217
Outtake: Parent/Teacher Relationships   220
Ages and Stages   220

Chapter 11: The Un-mentionables

The Money-Go-Round   229
Doing the Splits   234
The Inevitable Loss   237

Chapter 12: When Things Go Horribly, Horribly Wrong

Agonizing Apologies   244
Embarrassing Moments   245
Grace under Fire   246

Pet Peeves, A-to-Z   249
My Final Words   252
Test Your Etiquette Quotient: How
    Retentive Are You?   253
Acknowledgments   261
Lisa Gaché: Executive Biography   263
Your Own Personal Etiquette Journal   267

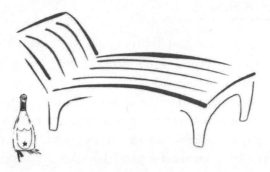

Introduction
Welcome to Beverly Hills

Everyone wants a piece of this town.

The relentless fascination with Beverly Hills didn't begin with *90210* or the now-famous housewives, but recently it's hit critical mass appeal.

I thought it was time someone came clean and revealed how the rich, famous, privileged, and entitled really behave in this little hamlet.

Although I am a native New Yorker, I nevertheless grew up in Beverly Hills, graduated from Beverly Hills High School, and still call it home. So I feel as though I've earned the right to own the subject.

I was raised in a somewhat non-traditional family, split by divorce. I can't say I wasn't privileged in many ways. Although we lived full time in a house on the wrong side of the tracks (in Beverly Hills, that means south of Wilshire Boulevard and east of Doheny—the *slums*) with my mother, my father would whisk my sister and me away on exotic vacations, and sometimes we'd ride in a chauffeur-driven limousine to school. But I was not reared with the good manners I teach today. I don't think I wrote a single thank-you note until I got married.

My two daughters were the impetus for my interest in this subject. I saw etiquette as an important foundation for becoming confident, self-reliant human beings, something I certainly wanted more of as an adult. I picked up this knowledge quite late in life, and it's a constant learning process. I hope this admission makes me, and the manners I'm teaching, more accessible to beginners.

I obtained my first job after college in the entertainment industry, working in music and film. Little did I know this entrée into that unique world would be the perfect foundation for my future work. My first foray as an entrepreneur was starting a concierge service, and I spent my time serving the big personalities in entertainment and the Internet, celebrities and CEOs alike.

My concierge business turned into a baby concierge business (if you've seen the Bravo show *Pregnant in High Heels*, that's it, in essence, sans the storefront and designer maternity line) after the birth of my second daughter. While doing research for my clients, I came across a class called "Petite Protocol" that was held at the Hotel Bel-Air. I called the hotel and had a lengthy discussion with their PR person, who suggested I scrap the concierge business and focus on forming an etiquette business because she felt it was a field that had not been saturated here in LA and yet was so needed, especially for children.

She connected me to the instructor of the class, etiquette expert Diane Diehl, who had more than twenty-five years of experience in the business and graciously took me under her wing and taught me everything she knew. Two years later, I was ready to open up my own shingle and founded Beverly Hills Manners, with the philosophy of teaching manners in a fun and entertaining way to bring these skills to a wider audience. In January 2009, the *Los Angeles Times* named us the etiquette school that will "teach your kids to be polite."

Even though I was receiving acknowledgment from the outside and had a wealth of hands-on experience, I felt it was important to have a credential to hang on my wall, so I enrolled in The Protocol School of Washington, the first and only nationally accredited school to meet the high standards set by the Accrediting Council for Continuing Education and Training (ACCET) and the US Department of Education. I received a certification as a Corporate Etiquette and International Protocol Consultant. The training provided me with amazing tools, as well as a few secrets I like to keep up my sleeve, which I am reserving purposefully so that even if you read this book cover to cover, you'll still have a reason to come to Beverly Hills and work with me in person.

Since then, I've had a blast dispensing tips on a host of local and national television shows. I've advised how to navigate public transit with ease and make a New Year's Eve toast to Anderson Cooper's guests, talked air travel perils with Kathie Lee and Hoda (and P.S., there were no formal offerings of alcoholic beverages), sorted through moral compass questions with *The Today Show* hosts, and counseled a loud-mouthed grandma who was making a public nuisance of herself at her grandkids' Little League games on Dr. Phil.

I receive regular inquiries spanning the continents, from Dubai to Hong Kong to Rio de Janeiro. They want to learn the ins and outs of how we do things here—to be *Americanized*, which is surprising to me, since Americans are renowned throughout the world as rude.

Not a day goes by without me having to dispel the many misperceptions about manners. I hear push back from parents and others who refer to etiquette class as a threat or punishment for bad behavior. Most believe this entire subject matter to be elitist and only for the extremely wealthy. While it's true that these rules were written for the upper crust, it's rarely the upper crust that practices them. A thoughtful upbringing can come from any strata of society. However, if you practice good manners, everyone will think you come from money, or the American South—minus an accent, a.k.a. *money*. Southern culture is a microclimate where most people are raised with exemplary manners, and I think southerners have a lot to teach other Americans in this regard. Everyone should have access to this information because it gives us such an advantage in human transactions, from the business world to traveling the world.

That world is changing every day, but the basic guidelines for mutual human respect are not. Whether you're five or ninety-five, any tools that enable you to feel more confident, poised, intelligent, communicative, and comfortable are of incredible value.

Welcome to Beverly Hills

Where narcissism is a competitive sport.

In this land of spray tans, designer rip-offs, surgical *enhancements*, and countless other hilarious, vacuous pursuits, the infatuation with celebrity lifestyles is more like a mass stalking. In general, celebrities are not helping. Reality (a word I apply with a second helping of irony) television rules the world now, and the more devastating the train wreck, the better. Why be polite and demure when *outrageous* is so much more tantalizing—and lucrative? A good scandal used to take weeks to unfold; now it's minutes, thanks to unsocial media. Still, the financial return on infamy is colossal, and it better be, because a shack in this zip code will set you back a couple mill. This is what we're exporting to the world: a cargo ship packed with bad manners, in very pretty packages.

And the world is buying it, by the bucket load.

These extremes of behavior are celebrated anywhere you can get WiFi. To battle this pandemic, we need to go back go to the source, the fertile crescent of rebellion against even the basic rules of etiquette. And I am referring to Crescent Drive, 90210. Swimming pools, movie stars, a place where a hillbilly can become a millionaire, and billionaires act like hillbillies. Your average hillbilly probably has better manners than most billionaires, and that's where I come in.

I understand the problem. In an age where everyone is rushing, pushing, and shoving to get ahead, each day is a breakneck race to accomplish the long list of ridiculous things we must do to get by. There's little time to address stresses, and apparently no time to stop, take a break, and consider others. The uncertain economy has left most people oscillating between fear and rage. We are all at the breaking point, really, due for a weekend in the rubber room. So, there are those who resort to pharmaceutical solutions to keep themselves from exploding at the insensitive, indifferent, and inappropriate responses that pelt us from every direction. And it's so much worse online, a free-for-all of insults and threats, under the veil of illusionary anonymity. Okay, breathe.

Most people cringe when they hear the words, "manners," "etiquette," or "civility."

But we're living in an extremely social world now, and really, what I teach is social skills. Manners have evolved to become vital navigational tools in this circus of human activity— years ago, a gentleman would walk curbside to protect a lady from the mud splatter from passing horse-and-buggies. That's not as crucial a gesture today (unless you winter back east, where a speeding SUV can spray you with red, salty mud if you're not careful).

> **The Golden Rule we teach children is timeless (and yet often ignored online): Treat others the way you would like to be treated.**

Until we are sealed in our own private bubbles, on a billion separate planets, live human interaction is necessary and for that, you need to be comfortable in your own skin, even in your worst moments. To make a good first impression, you still need a firm handshake and to look people in the eye. A handwritten thank-you note still beats a text. You would never show up to a friend's party without offering to contribute something, or let someone in need of assistance cross a busy street. "Please" and "thank you" still have power. So do "you're welcome" and "excuse me" and "I'm sorry."

Good manners are built on common sense, and common sense always tells you to be the least disruptive object in your environment. Calling attention to yourself can make you a target for predators, and we definitely live in a predatory world. No one needs any unexpected speed bumps to detain us from our insane schedules or bonus chaos to distract us from our profound thoughts. The goal, as ever, is to make your day more pleasant (as well as for those around you).

Good manners will inform the well-being of your relationships. These days toddlers text their parents and teens can skip schoolyard trauma, thanks to online communities. Courtship starts with what we used to call pornography, sexted instantly. But eventually you will find yourself face-to-face. What will you *say*?

Social anxiety comes from anticipating intimidating situations, real or imagined; social grace allows us to *deal* with intimidating situations, if they come up. It also gives us the confidence to interact with anyone, from A-list celebrities to someone threatening you for pocket change.

Once upon a time, etiquette revealed one's social stature. Now it reveals your *character*. Good manners level the playing field—your economic status is no longer an issue. This information can be yours, and it will take you anywhere you want to go.

The grace and sophistication you bring to every aspect of human conduct will do more for you than a shiny new car you can't afford or a million hours torturing yourself at the gym. Despite appearances, even in Beverly Hills, the observations about human interaction developed over centuries through trial and error still hold true. Conducting yourself in a manner that earns respect, rather than forces it, will get you much further than throwing temper tantrums.

Let's make every moment your best moment, shall we?

1

Keeping Up Appearances

You'll need to bring your best self to Beverly Hills. It doesn't matter if you're a hotshot real estate guru, a used Porsche salesman, or a "film producer" (lurking in coffee houses with a laptop, eavesdropping on conversations for ideas). Everyone here is competing for something—a multi-million dollar deal, CEO title, or the perfect, granite-hard gluts—and ambition is a flavor of adrenaline constantly flooding that saturated patch of your brain that governs illusions, delusions, and fantasies of success.

This competition may surface as a heated scramble for a parking space because you're late for a screening, or a war of wits over a minor role in a paper towel commercial to pay next month's rent. You may confront your chief competitor in the tennis club locker room wearing only a tiny towel and suddenly wish you'd spent more time on the elliptical machine—a lot more time.

No Second Chances: First Impressions, Lasting Impact

Let's get the unpleasantries out of the way first.

When you're going about your day, making a skinny double chocolate frappé run or say, getting an aromatherapy pedicure, the new faces you see—your friend Courtney's yoga partner, your agent's new assistant, even (especially) the nice young man who hands you a warm towelette at the salon—each has made a decision about you in approximately the first ten seconds of contact, before a single word has escaped your mouth.

These decisions are based on a package of subtle, but universal codes: your looks, your clothes, and your moves. Call it what you like—mojo, aura, energy, vibe—once that impression sets, it'll take a jackhammer and ten teamsters to dislodge it.

That's animal instinct, and we, as social animals, are always on the prowl for alphas (male or female) in the same way that in this town, you automatically scan a room for famous faces.

> *We're all on the hunt for the A-list, and that*
> *A stands for Animal Magnetism.*

Whether deliberate or otherwise, we are forever trying to discern our place in the larger hierarchy as a means of raising our status.

This is Beverly Hills. This is humanity, really. It's surprising we don't have tails. But we certainly have *claws*.

Fake It Until You Make It

What exactly is star quality? If you have it, you're familiar with the extended stares while strangers try to remember where they've seen you. *Is he on some TV show? Did I read about her in the* Vanity Fair *Hollywood issue?* Perhaps you do appear on television and in magazines, but it's your perfect balance of positive attitude and social ease that gives people this impression. Who cares if you're gorgeous, successful, or even employed? It's all about how you carry yourself in this world. It's all about the *intangibles.*

Poise, Confidence, Acting Skills

Even if your life is a rollicking shamble, you will show no evidence on your face. No one here wants to know about your wracking self-doubts or your hardscrabble childhood, your failing marriage or your corrosive political opinions. We came here for the sunshine, not the rain. Do your part.

But here's the plain truth, people. We are magnetic, molecular animals, and when others feel your ease, it puts them at ease. Your confident smile lets them know there are no leopards stalking in the tall grass. Or as the case may be, no stalkers in leopard skin boots and a handbag to match.

If you're relaxed among the A-list, even if you're not technically on that list, for all practical purposes, you will be A-list. Even if it's a ruse, enjoy it. That's what this place is all about.

Look the Part (or Someone Else Will Get It)

Whether you're in a generic metropolis or a posh community like Beverly Hills, it's not where you've come from (because half the town is from various places on the globe), it's who you want to be. And that's pretty much up to you. Here in the land of smoke, mirrors, and sketchy real estate deals, we create our own personas for recreation. This should serve as a warning about making snap judgments about people.

That guy handing the valet the keys to his $800,000 Lamborghini? He wants you to believe he's the prince of some rocky outcropping in the Mediterranean; in fact, he's an Albanian taxi driver spending his lottery money. That lady in ripped jeans stuffing her pony-like mutt into a Prius? Please address her as "Lady," because she's actually British royalty.

> ### *Perception beats reality, hands down, every time.*

The clothes you choose, your grooming habits, the language you use, the carefree way you go about your day—all of these choices reflect your aspirations. Who cares if you spent your high school afternoons working in the laundry room of a motel in rural Kansas? When you behave like a benevolent heiress, everyone from the breakfast maid to the head of Paramount Pictures will treat you like a benevolent heiress. We call this *grace*.

The more you act like the persona you aspire to be, the more likely reality will follow. In other words, it's your movie. You're the star and you get to cast the love interest and the minor roles, decorate the set, choose the costumes, and call action. In marketing terms, we call this *branding*.

You can turn your life around one hundred and eighty degrees, if you have the pluck and courage. . . .

> *I had a client who possessed fabulous looks, but arrived in Beverly Hills from a rather humble background. She was a self-confessed "trophy wife," who married a wealthy man many years her senior. Although it was a happy union, she felt uncomfortable around his often judg-*

mental friends, especially the ones down at the fabulously snotty country club. She pretty much spent her leisure time engaged in vengeance shopping. It took several sessions to build her confidence. I helped spruce up her posture, diction, and conversation skills and upped the level of elegance in her wardrobe. I also recommended she become involved in charitable work to give her life a deeper level of meaning. The outcome? She was ecstatic with her new self.

Wardrobe Malfunction!

Just don't tackle a disguise you can't pull off. There's a difference between good acting and flat-out lying about who you are.

Some of us are natural leaders in the art of crafting a personal brand, effortlessly choosing the clothes and decor and vehicles that become the perfect material projections of our self-image. Others are constantly reinventing their style based on the latest magazine spread they saw. Think you can't buy cool? Would it shock you to find out that the well-dressed woman over in the corner, talking to that gallery owner, pays six different advisors just to choose her shoes?

Nothing should surprise you here—especially the shotgun marriage of identity confusion and limitless resource.

If you go overboard, you'll feel like you're in drag, or worse, wearing a Halloween costume.

If you're not actually a dominatrix, a hip-hop star, or an eighties hair-rocker, eventually you'll get found out. The more your aspirations are in touch with your own personality and personal tastes, the better you'll move through this town, any town, and across this globe. Whatever your style, own it.

Body Language Needs No Translation App

Look alive! In the animal kingdom, the taller you stand, the less likely a predator will decide you are a snack worth risking a rumble. Imagine this town is a jungle, a jungle swarming with department store salespeople offering you night creams you don't need, hustlers wielding golf clubs, and man-eating divorcées looking for their next meal ticket.

Slouch at your own risk.

Yes, I blather on and on about "good posture." What I mean is this: Don't look small and helpless, like a frightened rabbit. It's the best way to avoid becoming someone's lunch. Walk as tall and straight as you can—if nothing else, you'll look thinner. Relax, it's a lot easier than trying to survive on maple syrup, cayenne pepper, and lemon water (what many Angelenos call "dinner").

Bonus Tip

Posture check! Stand against a wall with your heels touching the baseboard; your back, shoulders, and head should all be in contact with the wallpaper. Ladies: toes and heels together. Men: feet shoulder-width apart—that's the way to appear cool and confident, even if you're not. And it gets easier once you re-train your muscles.

Slow Down the Beat

Don't rush it, don't push it, don't run it over, and don't hurl yourself breathlessly to your next appointment. "Crazy busy" is the standard response to "how are you?" This is a transparent boast, disguised as a complaint. You might think you seem very, very important if you're always in a hurry, but you are communicating the exact opposite. This is a town where keeping others waiting seems to imply status (very wrongly, but that's another chapter).

If you're in a hurry, it means you're late and you *care*, which knocks you back several notches in the business hierarchy. It implies you work for someone else; in short, you're the *help*.

> *The more slowly you walk, the more power you convey.*

Act as though you have leisure time. Your show is on hiatus. You're waiting for your next big deal to seal. You are mulling over the purchase of a sweet French landscape painting or wondering which color of leather will best suit your new Range Rover's interior.

Slowing things down will also calm you in an intimidating situation, and this town is nothing if not an intimidating situation. Flailing, flustered, and working yourself into a panic increases your chance of making one of those *my God what have I done* errors.

Don't crash around like a delivery truck, unless you are, in fact, a delivery truck.

Ladies, walk lightly and carry a big handbag.

Gentlemen, don't shuffle down the sidewalk. Walk heel toe, heel toe with the weight evenly distributed across your feet. Shoulders down and back, suck in that intestinal tract, and push your collarbone out a bit. Unless this causes muscle tremors, you will appear assured as you walk into lunch at Soho House, alert and engaged—even if you're not. And that's helpful, given the way people run yellow lights here.

Bonus Tip

Calm down. In hectic and challenging circumstances, create an internal metronome on a very slow beat as you go about your maddening day. If it helps, think of a mellow, comfort-ballad in your head (Barry White, John Mayer, Coldplay, or whatever else suits your musical tastes), a gentle rhythm to soothe your soul during particularly trying moments.

How to Land Safely into a Chair

Every time I walk into a restaurant, I see a panorama of diners sunk into their seats like melting cookie dough, their chins almost touching the table. When sitting in the presence of others, make your approach at full height, and as you reach critical proximity, pivot and gently drop. After practice, this will become like flicking the autopilot switch.

Imagine you're a butterfly alighting on a rose petal, not a Boeing 747 crash-landing on a postage stamp.

Once seated, don't lean back and brace yourself with the chair's arms. Instead keep your back straight as a palm tree, your head high, and knees relaxed. And if you don't pay attention to your hands, soon you'll be utilizing them to fidget, play with your hair, feel for blemishes, or pull on your ears.

Ladies, stack your hands like pancakes, one top of the other, right over left. Cross your legs at the ankle, knees glued together. Even if you're sitting behind a desk—it's good practice and an excellent thigh strengthener.

Men, arms extended straight toward your knees. You'll be keeping both feet parallel on the floor, shoulder-width apart at all times, thank you.

Bonus Tip

All hands on deck. Gentlemen, please keep those hands out of your pockets in polite company. That's a convention dating back to the Wild West, when you might be hiding a lethal weapon in your pocket, ready to draw. Nowadays, keeping your hands stashed in your pockets is body language for, "I'm hiding something—hiding the fact that I'd rather be anywhere else!"

Outtake

How to Walk in High Heels

I'm four foot eleven and change—I *live* in heels. Lucky for me, platforms have made a comeback, because the comfort level is so much more sustainable. I even sport platform tennis shoes. Still, this isn't a walk in the park. There will be some discomfort; our job is to minimize that. Teenaged girls are wearing slippers to school, so it's no surprise that they're lining up to learn how to walk in heels for formal events! Here's what you need to know:

- Shoes vary wildly in size, arch, and width. So do your feet.
- The narrower the heel, the harder to balance.
- Don't optimistically overstuff, your reward will be pain.
- Types: Kitten, Wedge, Pump, Platform, Stiletto
  - Kitten heels start at 2.5 inches.
  - Stilettos can be a whopping 7 inches high, most are 4–5 inches.
  - The rest fall somewhere in between.
- Adjust for terrain. The most hazardous is cobblestone, and since half of Beverly Hills pretends it's a Tuscan city circa 1298, I'm on guard at all times. Also watch out for grates, grass, and carpet.
- Be realistic about how long and how far you'll have to walk when you're shopping in your shoe closet before an event.
- Open-toe heels demand regular pedicures.
- Find a good cobbler and up your street advantage by adding rubber dancing soles.
- A shoetree or wads of tissue will help your heels maintain shape between use.
- Feet should be cool and fresh, not hot and icky, when you slip them into $750 footwear.
- Point your toes when trying on heels and wiggle them to adjust.
- Stand up straight on both feet, holding supporting muscles tight.

- Make your first step with your right foot, land on your heel, and instantly shift weight to the ball of your foot to balance evenly.
- Repeat with your left foot.
- Now walk, heel-toe, heel-toe, like a swan on water, slow and methodical.
- Arms are relaxed by your side, and swinging effortlessly, opposite to your leg movement.
- Your hips should sway naturally and intentionally!
- At the end of a day, give your feet a hot soak, peppermint lotion, and slippers. A gift for a job well done!

Lights, Cameras, Close-ups, Oh My!

In a town where an inordinate amount of *oomph* is placed on appearances, it's difficult not to lose your mind trying to do a daily renovation on your body. Here, mirror time is approximately double that of normal people. It's no scandal to spend four hours at a gym each day or bore lunch pals with your raw carrot salad and kale-cracker cuisine, but there's a line. It's not that I desperately care about impressing people, but I know that any little advantage gives us a boost when the world seems devoted to crushing us for its own amusement.

You're a walking advertisement for . . . you.

Are we talking monthly Botox appointments or major machete work? Haven't tried it *yet*. I've done double takes on friends I hadn't seen for a while, because their painfully obvious plastic surgery has stretched and frozen their faces into lifeless, rigid porcelain plates. Blatant abuse of plastic surgeons is a zillion times more visible than your silly little laugh lines. However:

No. 1 in the Rules of Attraction is be . . .
attractive.

Okay, now you're mad. But attention must be paid. Because you never know whom you might run into at the valet: the latest Head of Development for "the next big thing"—whatever the next big thing is *this week*. Opportunities are loitering behind every door, window, and hedge here. A chance meeting at a party can alter the course of your life for the fabulous. Arrive at a scheduled business meeting in attire more appropriate to a party and you have just condemned yourself to something called minimum wage. *You never know.*

You might decide to make a run to Pinkberry in your coffee-stained hoodie, thinking, *I won't run into anyone I know at this hour*. Too bad you ran right into your future husband—in some other lifetime.

Not in this one, honey.

Clip It, Clean It, but Don't Cause Injury

You would not believe what I hear in the non-privacy of the beauty salon about the latest trends in hair care, and I'm not talking about your bangs.

Yes, I am going to use the term "manscaping," so let's get it out of the way right now. You may be expecting me to advocate a thorough process of shaving, waxing, threading, clipping, and buffing, to the point that both men and women are as smooth as snakes. To that, I say *no*. Men need a little something to separate themselves from the ladies, so please don't spend more mirror time on yourself than the girls.

It's one thing if your golf ball lands in the rough, but there's no reason to resurface your entire body as though a putting green.

That's too much pain for too little gain. In any case, before this conversation becomes more distasteful than it already is, let me simply advise you to take a full inventory of yourself from head to toe on a regular basis (weekly, if not daily). The hair that sprouts from your nose and ears, and that odd little mole that you really should have a dermatologist take a look at? Yes, those items require special instruments of torture, applied with skill and regularity. The most attention should be paid to your face and hands, as well as your feet (really, ever heard the phrase, "smells like a foot"?). Everything else is generally covered up by clothing, in other words, purely *extra-credit*.

When my hair behaves, all is right with the world. If not handled by a pro, my tresses become a frizzy mess.

The grass is always greener on the other side of the fence, and the same goes for hair envy. Appreciate what you've got. If you've been given a challenging mane, learn to work with your natural shrubbery or find someone who can. My hairdresser works only a few days a week, so my entire schedule revolves around her. A cut every couple months should suffice, and luckily, salons that specialize in just the blow-dry are popping up all over town.

If you color your hair, calculate how fast your roots become visible and plan accordingly. I'd advise you to book your appointments for the whole year in advance. If you can't afford to frequent the salon that often, then it's time to invest in a hat collection, pay a visit to the drugstore, or start accepting your shade *au naturel*.

Also, when my nails look like I've been changing the oil filter on my Mercedes—which I wouldn't even know how to do—it wrecks my whole day. The weekly manicure appointment, in addition to ensuring that my hands look presentable, helps me organize my routine.

Wipe Down All Exposed Surfaces

Unless you're on an excursion in the wild or visiting a Third-World disaster zone as a representative of a charity, there's no excuse for not bathing on a daily basis. Clean nails, effective but non-toxic anti-perspirant, a proper haircut . . . I'm stating the obvious.

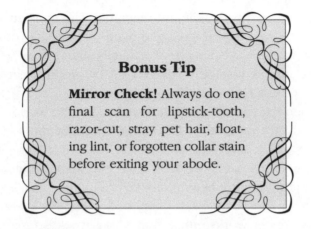

Bonus Tip

Mirror Check! Always do one final scan for lipstick-tooth, razor-cut, stray pet hair, floating lint, or forgotten collar stain before exiting your abode.

Let's get to a serious issue: sharing is to be admired, unless it's the flu and other viruses and bacteria. Even the finest Beverly Hills restaurant is likely riddled with microscopic bugs, although probably just on the saltshaker. If you have had any contact with children, you've already been exposed to nearly every virus known to mankind.

- Get in the habit of washing your hands with soap and hot water when you come home.
- Sub vitamin-C powder for soda when your energy starts sinking.
- Commit to garlic, the anti-viral, antibiotic, and anti-fungal wonder-stink.
- The minute you feel that mysterious, sudden exhaustion, cancel all appointments—you may be sick and contagious.
- Keep your feet, head, neck, and hands covered on freezing days.

- Carry a hand sanitizer for marathon meet and greets on the go.
- Sneezing? Coughing? Turn your head right, and expel into your elbow or a tissue or handkerchief or husband.
- Skip work if you're sick. Keep your sick kids home until symptom-free for at least twenty-four stir-crazy hours.

Keep Unsightly Habits Out of Sight

You may have a few nasty habits, and let's agree that you do, because everyone does. These might include, but are not limited to, nail-chewing, gum-snapping, knuckle-cracking, excessive hair-play, and worst of all, grooming of the extremely personal and unsanitary sort—public dental cleaning, irrigating of the ears, or visible nostril exploration.

Some distracting habits are appropriate in one setting, but not in another. I once had an assistant with very long hair that she enjoyed stroking in meetings. It was distracting to everyone and completely unprofessional. *Are we boring you, dear?* That's cute body language on a date, but not in a production meeting where we're discussing the budget for a $30 million film about teenaged robots in space.

Chewing gum is permissible—but only in secret—after a meal when you're unable to brush your teeth. It's best chewed in a hidden nook, for less than a minute, then discarded in an improvised wrap and deposited in a wastebasket.

I took on the mission of a self-obsessed, gum-chewing, single girl who wanted to land a royal husband. After an initial session of soul-searching and deep discovery, she finally realized that in this endeavor, she was her own worst enemy. We conducted an internal and external manners makeover, from her unconscious annoying habits and need to constantly interrupt, to the massive self-absorption that was preventing her from connecting on a more profound level with others. Realizing that she was the common denominator in the equation helped her to see the light and make a permanent positive change for the future.

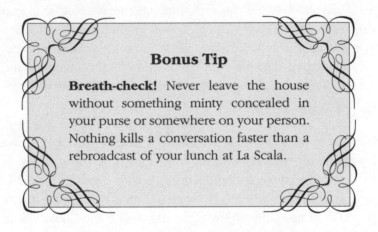

Bonus Tip

Breath-check! Never leave the house without something minty concealed in your purse or somewhere on your person. Nothing kills a conversation faster than a rebroadcast of your lunch at La Scala.

A Fashion Versus Style Smackdown

Oh, *fashion*. You can't even wear a long dress to an awards show without some bespectacled guy in a purple jacket and bow tie on a cable channel ripping it to shreds the next day.

Really, all a girl needs is a good blow-dry, a pair of fabulous heels, and a trench coat to protect her from the elements, and she's good to go. Your fur and feathers should consist of equal parts individual taste and common (good) sense. With all the makeover segments on morning shows, you'd think the message would be sinking in. My daughters are slowly beginning to grasp the concept, after years of listening to me complain when they would exit the house on a freezing day in shorts or try my patience by donning a miniskirt for a formal function without tights or stockings to cover their limbs.

> *Your choice of clothing is a weather vane*
> *that tells people whether you're taking off or*
> *grounded for life.*

A brightly colored ensemble announces, "I just scored a speaking gig at the convention center!" while that obscene t-shirt screams, "They impounded my car for too many parking tickets!" Here, *everything is career*, and there's no such thing as downtime. In a job interview, wear a suit unless it's with an Internet start-up where you would be mocked for choosing a new Banana Republic outfit. If you want a decent table at a restaurant, don't dress like a high school drug dealer, unless you're already a billionaire with a million friends on Facebook.

I get compliments about my appearance—along with a fair amount of teasing from friends and family—because I feel more comfortable in a dress suit than sweats. In truth, I'm a coat-fiend known for my expansive collection, which I wear just about every day of the week. A good coat will cover up almost any fashion crime (or a little modest tip of the scale).

> *Before a major shopping spree, I recommend*
> *you leaf through old embarrassing photos*
> *of yourself.*

You'll want to shred a few in the InSinkErator, cringing with horror, and I already know which ones—you're wearing something that was wildly trendy and probably set you back a week's paycheck. Some individuals can pull anything off, assembling fanciful outfits and outrageous accessories. These individuals are typically twenty-somethings with prepubescent figures or women who have wealthy spouses (and iron-clad pre-nups). Most of us aren't so lucky.

"Age appropriate" means nothing in Beverly Hills (and Southern California, in general), but I frown upon the stealing of your teenager's jeans (at your age, that's a plumber's crack, not a coin slot). Always present your best self, not the one that's desperately trying to rekindle a dead marriage. Even in that case, it's still more alluring to leave a few things to the imagination. You know what those things are.

Outtake

A Few Tips About Apparel

- Dress according to season, weather, and event.
- If the dry cleaner can't get the stain out, donate or toss.
- Showcase a look with clothes that fit your frame and shape.
- Tailors are less expensive than you might think.
- Add color seasonally (and like seasoning, sparingly).
- Jewelry, perfume—less is more, and even less than that is best.
- Neutrals are a sound investment—black, navy, brown, beige.
- A pair of dark jeans and classic blazer will get you almost anywhere.
- Graduate from detergent-faded sweat pants to a smart yoga outfit that can go to breakfast after class.
- Black is slimming—use it!

Ladies: These boring, unassuming articles of clothing will save your life.

- Black pant suit
- Black fitted pencil skirt
- Little black dress

- White button-down shirt
- Pumps in black and nude
- Black high boots
- Black purse

Men: Let everyone know you made it past eighth grade.

- Yes, you must own a suit, a good one
- Dark jeans can be dressed up or down
- V-neck sweaters for warmth
- Button-down shirts in white and blue
- Belts, brown and black
- Shoes, brown and black
- A decent-looking pair of sneakers, patent or suede, for more formal occasions
- If you must stand out, proportion item to extravagance—an expensive watch, an interesting tie, stylish shoes . . .

First I look at the Purse

They say you can tell a lot about a man by his shoes. I feel the same way about a gal and her handbag. Does she shun designer bags in favor of funky, affordable, sensible accessories? Or does she have the Hermés store on speed dial?

The well-groomed Beverly Hills woman will find it impossible to make do with one bag for all occasions. She will own multiples to choose from. She will recognize that one well-crafted quality bag will outlast five mediocre ones. She will understand that handbags are investments, and as such, will choose the classic over the trend.

Thanks to the knock-off shops, that $2,500 orange handbag you simply must have? In about a month, it will drop to $45 in a mall outlet shop.

The size of your bag should be of appropriate scale to your own size, as well as event. A large tote would look like a duffel bag on a petite lady such as myself. The higher profile the event, the smaller the bag. You'll require:

- A large tote for travel.
- A practical leather handbag in black/brown/beige for every day.
- A satin, silk, velvet, or beaded clutch in black or dyed to match a cocktail dress or coat for evenings out.
- A white or melon-colored handbag draped on a tanned arm, which looks spectacular in summer.

Overstuffing your purse with useless items is a mistake. You dig for your lipstick, only to come up dry—as though your purse contains a black hole to another dimension, one filled with all the items women have lost in their purses since the dawn of time. Just because your bag is big enough to contain your entire life doesn't mean it all belongs in there.

Outtake

Stash and Carry

- Carry your purse by the handles if it is a handbag or over the shoulder if it is a shoulder bag. Just make sure it's tucked out of the way when greeting newcomers with a handshake.
- At restaurants, keep your bag off the table, and avoid slinging it over your chair unless your back is to the wall.
- Best placement: first, a vacant chair; second, the floor, at your feet, to your left.
- Feng Shui dictates that a purse on the floor is "money out the door."
- If you object to sawdust, germs, and peanut shells touching your $2,500 handbag, then a purse hook is for you.
- A clutch can take a nap on your lap.

2

Pleased to Meet Me

By now we've covered the basics, so let's field-test your new skills. Challenging situations lurk around every corner. You might be invited to a post-premiere party filled with famous faces where you don't know a soul; a terrifying afternoon tea with a small group of aging supermodels who have all traveled the world; a forced march to a fundraiser for some reptilian political candidate and a round of knuckle-crushing and germ-smeared handshakes; or an evening at an uptight Beverly Hills restaurant with your work enemies watching to see if you know what to do with that teeny, tiny fish hook fork.

Despite the amazing race for material wealth in Beverly Hills, the most valuable treasure is largely hidden from view: *connections.* I arrived here nearly thirty years ago, and in that time I've been able to observe the rise and fall of those around me with the clinical eye of a research psychologist making a long-term study. Here's what I've learned: Careers are built on getting out and meeting people. Hiding in the safe haven of your gorgeous pad or luxury automobile won't get you jack. Those faces I consistently saw at parties and restaurants every night of the week? Now those faces appear regularly on television and in the *Hollywood Reporter*—in the movers and shakers section.

Successful socializing is built on simple, fundamental, age-old ideas: impressive introductions, engaging conversations, and well-orchestrated follow-ups.

Get out there and have fun!

If You Could Hear Yourself Talk . . .

In the world at large, the ability to make small talk with anyone, anywhere, is bankable. Even if it's just forecasting the weather or talking sports stats, most people like to think they're part of the world. Okay, except in this part of the world. This zip code probably contains the most distrustful people on Earth, because most people you meet here *want* something from you. Worse, public spaces are crawling with potential stalkers, climbers, paparazzi, and fans. Our closed loop—home, the car, the social circle, trusted restaurant—is our comfort zone. Most new acquaintances are made by mutual third parties and that means there's not a lot of off-the-cuff conversation (or social mobility). Instead, you'll probably only connect with new people at dinner parties or private events, via your existing friends who invited you and are vouching for your behavior and good graces. Do you like social pressure? Good.

Easy on the Ears

Some of us have been given the rare gift of a beautiful, sonorous speaking voice, each word sounding like heavenly harps or Yo-Yo Ma playing Bach on the cello. Others announce their presence with all the panache of a car alarm amplified through a nasal megaphone. If you grate, bray, screech, rasp, croak, bark, or squeak when you speak, consider the value of retraining your voice, possibly with the help of a professional. Otherwise every time you open your mouth, listeners are ignoring your vital message and instead frantically fishing for their noise-canceling headphones.

Ever snoozed through an otherwise fascinating talk because of the speaker's robotic monotone?

Or been driven crazy by a friend who turns every sentence into a question by skewing the last word an octave higher? Other aural crimes include squeezing words out of your pursing lips—you're not a saxophone—or spraying it, not saying it. Speed-talk makes you look like a nervous wreck (maybe you are). If you find yourself fighting for oxygen, you're probably hogging the conversation. And unless you're running a cattle call, which admittedly is a useful metaphor for most social interaction in this town, use your indoor voice. In other words, pump down the volume. You're so loud, you just made my cheese soufflé collapse.

Again, consider the law of the jungle. A deep, resonant voice implies power—use it! Think James Earl Jones as Mufasa in *The Lion King*. That should do the trick.

Language!

Allowing syllables to tangle up in your mouth like ramen noodles effectively obscures your message. Please don't butcher the pronunciation of words you've seen in print, unless you want to inadvertently amuse your listeners. Regular offenders include "inchoate," "debacle," and most French words. I was in line for frozen yogurt and the girl in front of me asked for "Grand Mar-in-er" (the flavor was Grand Marniér, and yes, only in a place like this do they offer liqueur-flavored fro-yo, and yes, I'd like one for myself, as well).

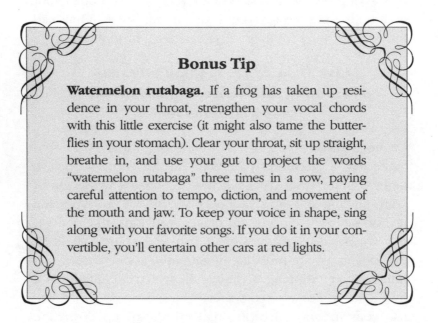

Bonus Tip

Watermelon rutabaga. If a frog has taken up residence in your throat, strengthen your vocal chords with this little exercise (it might also tame the butterflies in your stomach). Clear your throat, sit up straight, breathe in, and use your gut to project the words "watermelon rutabaga" three times in a row, paying careful attention to tempo, diction, and movement of the mouth and jaw. To keep your voice in shape, sing along with your favorite songs. If you do it in your convertible, you'll entertain other cars at red lights.

Misusing big words makes you look as silly as using baby talk.

In the same vein, unless you are writing a graduate-level thesis, the use of tortured academic language will only agonize the room. That's jet fuel for some people here—agonizing a room—but it shouldn't be for you.

The more succinct your message, the better chance others will listen.

Practice the art of articulation. Thanks to texting in lieu of talking, we're often tongue-tied in person. Fight this by reading out loud on a regular basis. Call in Mr. Shakespeare for those delicious rhythms or reinstitute the pleasure of reading books to your kids. And speaking of kids, have you noticed how they mumble? Kids look at the floor when they talk to you, apparently as an expression of *cool*. It is not cool. Your mumbling multiplies the probability that I will ignore your otherwise reasonable requests for snacks and new shoes.

Sometimes, language can be too vivid.

Unless you are addressing fellow actors, please don't make a habit of using foul language in public. The untimely release of an explicit expletive is no way to test the moral resilience of a new conversation partner. I would invite you to make the world a nicer place for children and other delicate souls by eliminating your banal cursing in favor of using new, more inventive phrases to express your indignation. That would be infinitely more intelligent than any dirty word you could think of.

Meet and Greet, Neat

An event's level of formality should guide your method of making introductions. Formal affairs include most social gatherings attended by VIPs (heads of state, heads of studios) and dignitaries (out-of-state politicians scrounging for entertainment money)—essentially anyone whose title exceeds "Mr." or "Mrs." Plus black-tie and dress-uniform parties (it's always awards season here!), or any work meeting featuring guests from outside the office (the investors from Texas or Qatar). Here's your cheat sheet:

- In a group, divide by alphabet—introduce A-list first (then B, then ignore)

- Ladies must be introduced to men, and not the other way around
- Younger people are introduced to older people
- For formal introductions always: "May I present . . ." and "How do you do?"
- Only in an informal gathering, you can use these old, well-worn shoes: "This is . . ." and "Nice to meet you."
- Greet dignitaries and your elders by their title and surname until given permission to do otherwise, "Please— call me Elton."

As this pageant unfolds (or degenerates into a schmoozefest, as the case may be), don't forget your basic body language cues. A nod lets someone know you're listening (unless you're actually nodding off). A smirk says, "Whatever, dude"—a most unwelcome sentiment whether issued verbally or bodily. Lean in and your partner will get the impression you're hanging on to every thrilling word as well as every dangling opportunity (thanks to Sheryl Sandberg).

Bonus Tip

Always stand to shake someone's hand. It's polite to stand for all introductions and farewells and when meeting someone older. It's a sign of deference, just as we stand to recite the Pledge of Allegiance or sing "The Star-Spangled Banner" or hail a hardworking B actor who finally gets an honorary award. The idea is to drop what you're doing and pay your respects on your feet.

And watch those hands, they tend to flail. Avoid folding your arms over your chest; it says, "Get me outta here!" in *neon*.

The Winning Handshake

Here's your shot. Take it. The initial handshake offers a little private moment where you have a chance to make a strong connection with someone new. Please program good handshake form into autopilot. I don't care if you're a renowned germaphobe—stash a hand sanitizer in your pocket. God help you if you refuse a handshake; such affronts are customarily settled by lawsuit. Who shakes whom?

* Defer to a VIP to initiate a handshake, as a sign of respect.
* A lady initiates, because a gentleman would never presume.
* In business, if it serves you to appear as the dominant party, be the first to thrust out your hand.
* Never, ever touch the Queen of England, or anyone from the A-list, for that matter.

Now you're ready to try it:

* From a standing, full-frontal position (if possible), establish solid eye contact.
* Smile that *new car smell* smile.
* Extend your right hand, your palm vertical, your thumb erect, and dive in wtih a firm handshake.
* Release tension to liberate your hand from a lengthy handshake.

Unless you are on some mutually agreed terms of intimacy (e.g., one of you has driven the other to Burbank Airport), please do not use your free hand to stroke the other's arm.

Here's a partial catalog of losing handshake styles I have experienced:

- *The Fluid Swap*—A damp palm reveals either sweaty social anxiety or worse, a recent trip to the loo, with a failure to make use of hankie or paper towel. Tip: A gentle swipe of the hands against your leg garments will remove any excess moisture.
- *The Blow-Off*—The obligatory quick brush that says, "I'm looking over your shoulder at someone more famous than you."
- *The Knuckle Cruncher*—You've just rendered my hand unusable for the next forty-five minutes. I'm not impressed with your manly power, I'm going into shock from the pain.
- *The Wet Noodle*—A limp, lifeless hand will cause your partner to sensibly run, in terror, thinking you've been in cold storage for the past twenty-four hours.
- *The Thumb Pincher*—Why are you digging your thumb into that sensitive nerve between my thumb and forefinger? If I wanted acupressure, I'd see Dr. Wu.
- *The Endless Handshake*—Let go of my hand. Now. Please. Let go. It's been ten minutes, this is getting weird, and I'm looking around for a security guard. (Relax your hand and your partner should get the message.)
- *The Shoulder Dislocation Dance*—Sometimes people get carried away with their *joie de vivre* and I understand that, but you're not fixing a flat tire and I'm not a spare jack, so don't take my rotator cuff for a spin with your exaggerated, full-arm handshake! Combined with a hug best reserved for the wrestling mat, I'm about to file a restraining order.

Whatever you do, avoid the inadvertent back slap at all costs. Remember the NFL debacle between the two Jims in 2011? San Francisco 49ers coach Jim Harbaugh and Detroit Lions coach Jim Schwartz had to be separated by players after a dust-up. The NFL network hired me to provide step-by-step instruction on shaking hands and good sportsmanship, in anticipation of their 2012 rematch on the field.

Eye-to-Eye

In an age where our gaze is often stupidly directed onto the screen of our smartphones, the daring act of looking someone in the eye seems archaic and perhaps frightening. Your eyes open a window into the soul; one glance can reveal whether someone seems trustworthy or suspicious (or *high*). It's a matter of survival. A steady, solid connection makes you seem more respectful and professional, while darting eyes will arouse anxiety and trigger an urge to seek shelter.

Always talk to someone as if he or she is the only person in the room. Avoiding eye contact or allowing your eyes to wander will make you seem rude, or worse, downright *shady*. Are you casing the joint for a robbery? Are you scanning the room for more interesting, important prey? In this town, people often seem primarily interested in other people as vehicles for their advancement. A quick word to careerists: The less obvious you are about this, the more likely you'll depart with the valuable digits.

Please Be Careful Not to Stare

Talking to a celebrity you really admire? First of all, don't do what I did when I met Barbra Streisand. Years ago, we were all waiting in line to be seated at a restaurant in Sun Valley. I made my approach, intending to simply shower her with accolades. I ended up showering her with tears of overwhelming emotion.

In the animal kingdom, staring is considered a lethal challenge. So break up your wide-eyed look of wonder with a few nods and shifts in your face angle. Also, monitor your blinking. Not enough and you look like you've gone off your meds; the same can be said for too *much* blinking. And finally, match your partner's demeanor—if they smile and laugh, you should, too. Fall into their rhythm, as though you were dancing, because this isn't a solo performance, this is a waltz (and if you're lucky, a sexy tango).

Be aware, however, that overseas, the rules are different. In Asian cultures, children and employees show respect by *avoiding* eye contact. Many Middle Eastern cultures feel eye contact between opposite sexes conveys an appalling lack of respect.

> ### *In this town, a condescending smile is ubiquitous, like knock-off Prada bags.*

Offer your winning smile, but don't *force* it, because a forced smile looks it. Plus excess smiling is annoying and often alarming. A smile doesn't always mean happy—a lot of us smile when we're angry. However, studies suggest that active smiling can actually trick your brain into sensations of happiness, which is helpful in combating social anxiety and other modern disorders. When you're stuck in traffic and ready to release a stream of expletives at the mindless drivers blocking you, try breaking into a wide, open-mouthed grin of wonder. You'll trick your animal brain into thinking you're at a party, sharing a Popsicle with Bradley Cooper.

> **Bonus Tip**
>
> **Smile workshop.** Hold a smile workshop in your bathroom mirror. Test-drive a smile that looks relaxed and natural, not like you're at the dentist's office preparing for a stinging teeth-whitening session.

Outtake

The Name Game

People get very funny about names, especially if you mispronounce or forget theirs. It's more than a case of respect. Name amnesia cuts down to the bone; to ego and self-image. In a town where everyone's trying to be a somebody, if you can't remember someone's name, you might as well just hand them a nametag that says: "Hello, my name is Nobody." If you continue to forget after multiple meetings, the message is clear: "You can't do anything to advance my career! Who invited you?" Nice. Here are a few tricks to avoid this common little faux pas.

- **Remembering names.** Use a mnemonic device, like a rhyme, to help remember.
- **Pronouncing names.** If there's going to be an issue, and you have advance warning, practice! If surprised by something exotic, asking them to repeat their name slowly might help.
- **Forgetting names.** It's allowed once and only once; after that, you're on your own. Be gracious when you say, "I'm sorry, please tell me your name again?"

- **Introducing a friend to a group.** Concoct a label for the group, "Samantha, these are the characters I lose buckets of money to on celebrity poker night; friends, this is Samantha."
- **Repetitive intros.** Keep track of introductions; re-introducing the same two people to each other, again and again, is on par with forgetting a name.
- **Unmemorable?** Don't keep them guessing. Reintroduce yourself with a smile.

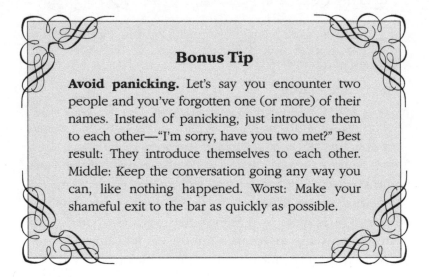

Bonus Tip

Avoid panicking. Let's say you encounter two people and you've forgotten one (or more) of their names. Instead of panicking, just introduce them to each other—"I'm sorry, have you two met?" Best result: They introduce themselves to each other. Middle: Keep the conversation going any way you can, like nothing happened. Worst: Make your shameful exit to the bar as quickly as possible.

Outtake

Addressing the Ladies

Here's a deficit in the English language we need to address: using "you guys" to address a group of girls. Why not, hey *girls*? I hear *hey lady* is coming back into style, which sounds amazingly fresh. But when did girls become guys? I have no idea, but it's a good time for a refresher on the variety of social titles appropriate to addressing a lady.

- **Mrs.** Traditionally, a woman's marital status dictated her social title. Mr. Ashton Kutcher's wife, Demi, became Mrs. Ashton Kutcher, until the (in this town, inevitable?) divorce, when she became Mrs. Demi Kutcher. Well, in her case, Demi Moore.
- **Ms.** Given to single or married women, the women's liberation movement in the seventies spawned this hybrid title to give women their own version of Mr. Use it when in doubt or anytime you feel nostalgic for the Me Decade.
- **Miss.** A conventional term of respect, Miss Daisy. A girl fifteen or younger still gets called Miss; some unmarried women prefer the term. The dance world has incorporated the term for instructors, followed by first names. Miss America, Miss Transgender Universe, Miss Understood, and Miss Conception . . . this little word isn't going away.
- **Ma'am.** A term mostly associated with the south, as a show of courtesy and respect. It's drifted into a term for older, matronly women, with some resistance. You'll know exactly what I'm talking about the first time someone uses it on you.
- **Madam or Madame.** This title is reserved to politely address a French woman whether she is married or unmarried. It is the equivalent of using the titles Mrs. or Ms. It's also what you call a female cabinet secretary—"Madam Secretary," as well as the wife of a foreign dignitary and the female head honcho at a certain kind of social club.

Smack! Incoming Air Kiss

As ammo for any meet and greet, don't forget your breath mints, just in case there's someone from Europe in the crowd. Americans are typically reticent with the kissing unless they've enjoyed a stint abroad. Once one person initiates an air-kiss greeting, everyone will enthusiastically jump in. Here, a proper air kiss begins with the right cheek first, hands lightly touching shoulders, lips never touching the skin. Get out quick! In France, friends and family hit both cheeks, right and then left. In Belgium, it's three air kisses—right, left, right. In Austria and Italy, air kisses on both cheeks are exchanged only after people become familiar. In England, one or two, depending, I guess, on how each party feels about looking French. In the Middle East, men kissing each other on the cheek is a standard greeting, but it's never applied to greeting women. Indians refrain from such public displays.

Bonus Tip

Celebrity contact. Here in the Hills of Beverly, you're likely to encounter individuals who have attained stellar levels of success. Don't heap on the flattery; no one likes a sycophant. Reciting their résumé will bore them instantly; they already know what they've done. And since these individuals are generally flesh and blood humans, they tend to amount to more than just their career (with some notable exceptions). In fact, talking about anything but their career success will be refreshing.

3

Indirect Communications

Really, what you do with your life is your business. Job interviews are yours to blow, a business dinner is a fun way to disgrace yourself, and an international meeting provides the best setting to insult a client. Unfortunately, Twitter and Facebook mean private mistakes can quickly become public. Submit a photo or tweet while intoxicated? Digital means forever, so if that photo goes viral, you will be dealing with a fast-moving pyramid scheme of shame.

In Beverly Hills, your worst moments can also be caught on video, replayed on TMZ or YouTube a million times, featured on every major news outlet, and then developed into a reality television show. Okay, that's true of anywhere in the world now. But here, the likelihood is so much higher because the locals, the paparazzi, and the tourists are all on the lookout for a celebrity moment. And they all have cameras. You do not want those cameras aimed at you.

A Word about Privacy

Years before I started teaching etiquette, I worked in the entertainment industry in business and legal affairs. How could I have known that training would be so useful now? Every day, the job hammered home the importance of using precise language to preempt potential disasters. Thanks to technology, now all of us need to become our own one-stop legal affairs office.

Privacy is life or death in this little burg, and it's guarded accordingly.

Expect Rottweilers, rent-a-cops, and a team of attorneys bearing restraining orders. During the golden age of Hollywood, studios erected multiple layers of ironclad insulation to protect actors from the masses. However, social media has erased that buffer zone. The famous are *expected* to communicate directly with their fans, or at least give this impression (through their little army of smiling assistants).

More and more, this strategy is failing as celebrities go rogue, releasing incendiary thought-bombs that reveal blazing ignorance and failure to use spellcheck. Even the smartest guard dog is short on grammar skills, and the best spin-doctors can't mop up the mess caused by an embarrassing tweet or photo that blows up like a flu virus in a crowded international airport. Digital is forever. Mistakes, now permanent.

Privacy no longer exists—for any of us.

In truth, it never did. We are social animals, always watching each other. Many of us have embraced a cornucopia of bad habits online (narcissism, voyeurism et al.), believing—incorrectly—that our anonymity creates a layer of insulation from consequence. Looking for a job? Meet someone amazing? Your prospective employer or dinner date can easily find that embarrassing party photo, those vicious words you posted about your ex, the online feud with a co-worker, or that vulgar tweet you issued after imbibing a few too many. Think before you hit "send."

In the Digital Age, we're all under surveillance.

It's like we're all celebrities.

We also seem to believe that each new advance on the "Net" creates a new rule of etiquette. I would disagree. Apply the same rules of etiquette online that guide you in face-to-face conversations and you'll avoid trouble. In person, we try not to bully or shout. In person, we allow others to express themselves. If we become annoyed with someone, we make a quiet exit. Etiquette is etiquette. To repeat, it's about being a thoughtful, considerate individual who socializes with ease, draws attention away from oneself, and celebrates a graceful, sophisticated viewpoint of life. And that will never change, whether you're online or off.

Telephony

Have you noticed that some people have completely given up using their phones to *talk*? What do you think "unlimited minutes" means? It's become almost rude to call someone without a pressing reason. It's a silly truism, especially because a simple call can solve a problem in seconds that a furious, thumb-intensive text exchange takes a whole afternoon to accomplish. Still, the phone will ring and you will pick it up. Know what to do.

Outgoing calls:

- Good manners dictate that social calls should generally be placed between 7 a.m. and 7 p.m., later on weekends. Do avoid calling during family dinner hour.
- If you must deviate from these time windows, remember to apologize for the hour. Particularly if you've just looked at the time and it's 3 a.m.
- Identify yourself, and ask if it's a good time to call.
- Have a specific reason to call, get your business done, and then you can chat if the recipient is willing.
- Smile when you talk—you'd be surprised how your pearly whites travel across the phone connection.

Incoming calls:

- Some prefer the informal *hellos*, but others break it out to, "Hello, you've reached the Hickenbacher residence." It's a family decision.
- If you need to track down the desired recipient, don't shout like an extreme makeover coach. Place the caller on hold or say, "Just a moment please, I'll see if he/she is home."
- If not, your response should be, "He/she is unavailable at the moment," and then take a detailed message.
- In a chaotic household with multiple members, always have message paper and pen handy, as well as a central location to post messages.
- **Call waiting.** A lovely feature, designed to suspend a current call and switch to a new incoming call, provides a fresh opportunity for confusion. Take the call and you've just created an instant hierarchy, and no one likes to know he or she is your second choice. Fend this

off by warning a conversation partner in advance that an urgent call may be coming in. Your options (all bad):

- Let your current phone partner know you'll be right back and quickly dispense the new incoming call.

- Let your current phone partner know this incoming call is urgent (your mother, for example, whether this reflects reality or not) and you'll call them back.

- Let the call go to voicemail; honey, that's what it's for.

- **Speakerphones.** This option offers another effective way to annoy your caller. Have a reasonable excuse for putting someone on the box, and always ask permission. Sometimes it's difficult to hear using these devices, so if the situation is reversed, you can blame your own phone equipment and ask to be taken off speakerphone. If you're driving and there are kids in the car, warn your incoming caller immediately before they begin a bashing session filled with expletives meant for adult ears only.

- **Ending a call.** Sometimes easier said than done. As a rule, assume others have busy lives and their time is precious. Don't linger on calls if business concludes. Some of us are sad and lonely and abuse call time as a substitute for actual human contact. Others love the sound of their voices so much, they never tire of them, even as you work your way down a list of household chores that you can manage with one hand (or using speakerphone!). Advances in mobile phone adapters for cars exacerbate this problem, because some commuters turn car time into call time. The person who initiates the call should also be the determinant to end the call.

- **Voicemail messages.** These should be short and to the point. Avoid leaving cryptic words that might arouse anxiety ("This is your attorney's office, please call us at your soonest possible convenience!"). And steer clear of leaving confidential or incriminating messages for someone's assistant to hear and later tweet. And no hang-ups. It's so disconcerting. Learn to leave a detailed message.

- **Screening calls and returning calls.** Sure, avoid the call. Again and again. Of course, that doubles the chances you'll run into Miss d'Call in the line for dollar/minute massages at Whole Foods. You should return calls within twenty-four hours, unless you're out of town. Hate to return calls? Leave town a lot.

- **Wrong numbers.** Be nice. The caller has your number.

- **Telemarketers.** I know you're tempted to chew out that caller. Do you imagine the caller aspired to a telemarketing job where 99 out of a 100 calls yield an irate and sometimes vicious response? No, he or she took that job because he or she has just found out that fifty is the new sixty in the business world and is slipping on the mortgage. Have a heart and surprise the caller with a gentle, "No, thank you."

- **Distracting noises.** It's ridiculous that I must mention that it's impossibly repulsive to munch a snack or use the restroom during a call, but the practice has persisted since the invention of the cordless phone. Also, you could explode someone's eardrum by sneezing loudly into the receiver.

- **Focus!** Please don't waste others' precious time in an effort to join the multi-tasking revolution. In other words, don't surf the net while you're on the phone; your inattention is audible.

Bonus Tip

Beverly Hills callbacks. There's a local way of doing business here that always surprises out-of-towners. Let's say, you receive a job referral from a friend to work for a Mr. Solomon. You place the call to Mr. Solomon's office and leave a message. And it isn't returned. This is normal, I'm sorry to say. Your second call won't be returned, either. Your third call is actually to let Mr. Solomon know that you're serious and you will be calling again. Your eventual returned call will be made by a cheerful assistant who assures you that Mr. Solomon received your message and will be returning your call in the future. That callback will be issued at a time when it's certain that you won't be available—typically at lunch or after hours around 8 p.m. Your most probable way of connecting with Mr. Solomon, therefore, is running into him at the tennis club. Buy a racket.

Mind Your Mobile Manners

Mobile technology provides us with a new set of distractions and ways to put our attention deficits on public display. The act of making ourselves available to receive communications twenty-four hours a day also brings with it twenty-four hours of random interruptions. No one likes being ignored. When your caustic little handheld device issues an annoying alert, you must often choose between offending whoever is calling/texting/tweeting you, or whomever you're socializing or conducting business with. Marvelous idea, this mobile technology!

- **Vibration mode.** Go silent in public places. The urgent grunt of your phone in vibration mode is just as jarring as a ring—particularly because everyone else has their phone on vibration mode and just reached for their phones, too.
- **Important/urgent calls.** Take them, but if possible, warn your companions ahead of time that you may be receiving impending calls.
- **Mealtime.** No, don't place your phone on the table. Keep it in your lap, if you must. Do I have to ask you to avoid initiating text wars at the dinner table? Apparently I do.
- **In public, at events** . . . Oh my goodness, a loud conversation in a public place on a mobile phone is a very intrusive kind of over-sharing. Understand, it may be true that everyone knows everyone and everything about everyone, but don't contribute to it. Please.
- **At the movies.** Here, we call them "screenings." And everyone in the room believes that their important business far outweighs the artistic integrity of the director, actors, and various artisans involved in the making of the film. And that pretty much explains this town, in a nutshell.
- **Accidental dialing.** Lock that screen before stuffing your phone in your back pocket. I do not want to know the less-than-glowing remarks you might make about me behind my (your) back.
- **Dropped calls.** Let's establish this, once and for all time: Whoever made the call is responsible for calling back after a dropped call. This will eliminate the busy signal when both parties try to reconnect.

Texting and Subtexting

For some, it's the perfect solution to a busy schedule. For others, the scourge of contemporary life. Everywhere we go, we invariably hear that persistent little tone. Hey, at least we're starting to use different text alerts. Watching everyone grab for their pockets and purses when one goes off in a crowded lunch spot is high comedy in modern America.

The awkward keyboards on our mobile devices, compounded by the operation of such devices while in motion, makes for flippant retorts, accidental filler, faulty grammar, and atrocious spelling. And it takes eight exchanges to say goodbye. In that time, you could have read your weekend script assignment. In short, our state-of-the-art technology has turned us into one-note simpletons.

I'm a fan of brevity, but not incomprehensible shorthand.

Between the made-up abbreviations and verbless non-sentences, sometimes *I just don't understand what you're saying*. And don't flip out if someone doesn't return your text. I silence my phone whenever I'm at an event, or lunch, or don't feel like working my thumbs. Texting while driving, walking, or talking to someone else isn't just rude, it's dangerous.

Texting is ideal for communicating when we find ourselves in noisy rooms. It's perfect for letting someone know you're running late or waiting in the back booth at the restaurant. Texting is, however, absolutely useless for expressing complex emotions. And this is my major criticism of the most infuriating of all the new global tech tools.

A serious relationship cannot be conducted on a tiny smartphone screen.

Texting is a particularly inappropriate platform for breaking up with someone, and yet, apparently, that's how our callow, callous youth conducts affairs. Fine. As a mother, I'm wary of teenagers getting into serious relationships. But I defy you to pursue a serious relationship while using "U" for "You," unless you are Prince and it's the 1980s. Texting gives us the impression of constant spontaneity, but also that commitment is optional. It is not.

Worse, sending a private, intimate message that appears in full view, on a device that can be displayed to a crowd, is ill-advised socially and otherwise. That text you just sent, trashing someone in your circle? It just appeared, in full, on the lock screen of your recipient's smartphone, which is sitting face-up on a restaurant table, surrounded by that same circle, all of whom glanced over at the alert sound and read it. Oops.

I love the way ultramodern humans have reverted to the most antiquated form of communication— the written word.

Old-Fashioned Email

By now it seems like email has been around as long as the horse and buggy. In a way, it has. Email has resurrected the wonderful tradition of fervent correspondence, a centuries-old passion temporarily killed by the reliance on telephones.

Spending hours on the phone with the object of your affection is thrilling, but so is receiving a highly anticipated, beautifully written email. (Okay, a letter is better, but email's quicker!)

In any case, email's been around long enough that I'll assume you are aware of rookie errors. Like not knowing that using all caps means you're *shouting* at someone. And we could probably keep a campfire going all night with horror stories spawned from accidentally hitting "reply all." Here are some other basic rules for keeping your email relationships in good stead:

- Return emails within twenty-four to forty-eight hours.
- If you're concerned you may forget, designate a regular hour each day to returning emails.
- If you are pressed for time but want to respond in full, send a quick note explaining the situation.
- Please utilize the subject line, as though you would label a folder. This is an invaluable help when you're searching, months later.
- Check your spam folder regularly in case of an over-eager filter.
- BCC, not CC. Never share your contacts' email addresses with the mob.
- Insert that smiley face if you're not sure your humor is painfully obvious.
- Use spellcheck!

Bonus Tip

Unbalanced email relationships. Sometimes we are pelted by long, confessional impromptu novels and do not feel a desire to do the same. Good manners dictate that we be sensitive to others' needs, including our own. As with any uneven relationship, your job is to gently restore equilibrium by slowing down and shortening your response, without being curt or cruel. We hope your partner will get the message and follow suit.

- Privacy reminder: Don't write anything that you wouldn't want everyone to read. That "forward" button is just one click away.

Get It Right in Writing

Oh, the long, beautifully written letter, every word aching with meaning, meant to be read and re-read, again and again—disappearing in favor of short buzz-phrases issued on the fly, while driving? I wonder. Aware of the possibility of mass distribution, we often edit intimate thoughts from our text messages. All that's left is flip, empty, entertaining sound bites.

I urge you to commit, in writing, to your relationships. Learn to really communicate, in words. Return to the habit of thinking in full sentences that contain complex, interesting thoughts. Whether it's for work or play, you'll be pleased with the results.

> *Don't you think it odd we don't recognize each other by our handwriting anymore?*

Sure, we're all such fast typists now, but we have no idea what our closest friends' handwriting looks like. Once upon a time, handwriting analysts had healthy careers, psychoanalyzing people by simply noting how they slanted their capital letters or dotted their i's. We learned to rely on the written "voice" for such insights into personality, because handwriting offers such deep and revealing clues. And that's definitely a disadvantage.

> *I'm a fierce advocate for snail mail.*

Support the US Postal Service

The deficit left by digital transmission may actually increase the value of a hand-written message. Letters arrive sealed, to your door, for you and only you to open. After you read it, you can burn it, making the words a secret, forever, between two people. Or you can stash it in your underwear drawer or file it in a trunk filled with other memorabilia, and your grandkids can read it, long after you're gone, and marvel at how romantic you were in your youth, you old thing.

It's such a luxury to find a personal letter or the new issue of *Etiquette Weekly* in my mailbox (along with, granted, invitations to accrue debt, coupon advertisements, and votes for local politicians). Many have discarded the form as an ecological choice. (But do you honestly have any idea what happens to your three-year-old computer processor when you discard it?) It's time to revive the tradition.

Find yourself some dignified stationery or create your own. Go all out and locate your local letterpress for notes, cards, and letterhead that make a powerful statement of elegance. Put the date in the upper right-hand corner, and let it rip with the sentiment, the beauty of the written word, and the liberating vulnerability of releasing your deepest thoughts. Then reread it for grammar, spelling, and easily misinterpreted statements. When you mail it, you've said more about your relationship than any quickly dashed-off email, accidentally copied to six work colleagues, ever could.

Thank You for Writing a Thank-You Note
Certainly, someone, somewhere, sometime will perform some act of kindness toward you in this lifetime. They might give you a fantastically personalized birthday gift. Make some grand public gesture of which you are the lucky beneficiary. Invite you to hang out at a coveted Malibu Colony beach house on the Fourth of July. Consent to interview you for a dream job with some record producer. Share box seats to see the Lakers playoffs. Whisk you away to a celebutant dinner at Mr. Chow's. Save your big toe from frostbite in an

Aspen ski-slope emergency room, or recommend your kid for entry into a competitive nursery school in Brentwood. All of these un-random acts of kindness and superhuman professional gestures require a formal response.

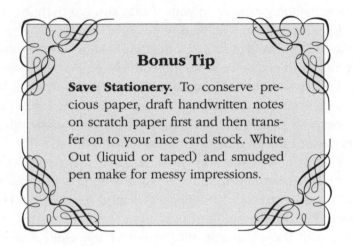

Bonus Tip

Save Stationery. To conserve precious paper, draft handwritten notes on scratch paper first and then transfer on to your nice card stock. White Out (liquid or taped) and smudged pen make for messy impressions.

Once this event takes place, the clock starts ticking.

You have less than forty-eight hours to compose a proper thank-you note. Certainly, it's not completely incorrect to acknowledge small gifts and favors via email, but if you're with me—really *with* me—you will see the wisdom of keeping an address book, online or otherwise, complete with mailing zip codes, and you will send a handwritten thank you. An email is second-best, at best, and sometimes the only way to properly address a large group thank you. A text is fine as an immediate response after an impromptu evening or other minor deeds.

Here's the anatomy of a thank-you note:

- The actual words "thank you," once at the beginning, and again at the end.
- Mention the gift, event, or act of kindness rendered and how it benefited you.
- Include a unique detail that will add sizzle and spark to the connection.

Please don't make it look like you dashed this off while being suspended over a tank of piranhas with a pistol pointed at your forehead. It may end up on the family mantle for a week or more, read by others, or even tucked into a scrapbook. With that in mind, use your best handwriting and make sure the note and envelope are free of coffee stains, et cetera.

Get in the habit of sending thank yous, and you'll be amazed at how your friends will continue to include you in events, remember birthdays, and do unasked favors for you. Also consider gift baskets, freshly baked gluten-free muffins, handmade bars of French soap, and other tokens of gratitude when someone really goes the extra mile.

Unsocial Media
View it for what it is, my Facebook friends and Twitter and Instagram followers: an *addiction.* You drop everything, every forty seconds, to check for new messages, new tweets, new photos and posts! Add the relentless ringing of the phone, plus all your friends and family and job pressures to this combo plate, and it's no wonder that you're getting indigestion.

> ***Real people hate to be ignored.***

Yes, those would be the friends who deliver chicken soup when you're sick and babysit in emergencies without complaint. The friends you fall back on when the flock turns on you. Not the friends who send YouTube clips of celebrities falling and links to sketchy diet products. So please, refrain from paying more attention to your digital life at the expense of your *real* one.

Sometimes we do develop deep and healing relationships with like-minded online groups. Or juggle multiple online personalities, as part of a predatory dating scheme. Whatever it is, I'm not interested in your personal life. I *am* here to advise you to guarantee the security of your professional life (and family life) by paying attention to the trail of breadcrumbs you leave online.

Use these tools wisely to enhance your life, not enslave it.

Your online experiences can become tremendous assets, an exchange of knowledge, of support. Just be sure to disconnect from the matrix on a regular basis and reconnect with the most important people in your world: you and your actual loved ones. Spend your precious time investing in your future and your passions.

Tweet Me? Tweet You!

In the beginning, Twitter was a new, distilled form of communication, namely 140 characters that answered the unsolicited question: *What are you doing right now?* Users would tweet mundane musings about breakfast cereals and yoga positions. But Twitter evolved at quantum speed, and eventually became usurped by self-promoters, as both a marketing tool and a useful live newsfeed from the ground zeroes of the latest disasters—metaphorically, as well as literally. The best tweets seek to enlighten, educate, and entertain. Oh, but how this remarkable little tool can go so wrong, so fast.

As with any act of self-promotion, a thoughtless tweet can dramatically backfire.

Under the excitement of immediacy, users are tricked into hitting the "tweet" button without double and triple and quadruple checking. Factor in the awkward smartphone keyboards that make spelling and grammar violations easy, plus the fact that you're at a noisy party and have consumed six different variations of a martini. Suddenly, Twitter can turn a minor, local commotion into a global gaffe. *Why did I just tweet that?* Bad news travels fast, junior high–style. Politicians, sports figures, and entertainment celebrities are going down right and left—and the public loves it. Upload a risqué photo or unnecessarily catty comment and you will hit the embarrassment jackpot, too. It's as though the digital world gives us permission to be bratty children. If you wouldn't say it to someone's face, or want your grandmother to read it, don't tweet it!

I post on @90210manners. The best way to avoid Twitter wars is to restrict your tweets to positive thoughts, brilliantly stated, which, P.S., will make you sound more intelligent than any bitter, ill-worded putdown. Here are a few things to remember when you launch that app:

- Don't tweet when you're angry, drunk, or have had way too many espressos.
- Utilize all necessary precautions if you spell like a seven-year-old.
- Avoid childish insults, vulgar insinuations, and libelous claims.
- Know the difference between a direct message and a tweet to your entire list of followers. For details, ask *former* Congressman Anthony Wiener.

Killing Time on Facebook

First of all, do bear in mind that you are the content Facebook uses to make money (in the billions, whatever it is, today). Did you get your check? I didn't get mine. Granted, thanks to Facebook, we can reconnect with old friends and make new ones, all with one click, keeping on top of our social lives as never before. Also, thanks to Facebook, we've become a nation of loafers and voyeurs.

Ever wonder why the economy continues to be so sluggish? Some days I believe it's because of all the time we spend on Facebook. Think of those endless debilitating hours lost in absorbing the trivial pursuits of your friends instead of working overtime for a promotion, fixing up your house, or engaging in cardiovascular exercise. Before the invention of this dazzling technology, exposure to this sort of material was limited to furtive whispers or filtered through the *grapevine*.

Facebook encourages us to believe we are fascinating.

In this culture of self-congratulatory joy, we are assaulted with every inane detail of our friends' comings and goings. To me, it sounds like we're inventing new ways to say the same message, over and over again: "Look at what *I'm* doing, *I'm* so cool."

Understand that every time you say that, you might also be unintentionally saying: "And you're not!"

View Facebook as a great way to stay in touch with friends and find out what's happening Friday night. And remember, sometimes a little mystery is your greatest asset. Otherwise:

• If you are touting an achievement, please deflect the blatant self-promotion by thanking anyone who helped you. Self-deprecation also goes a long way.

- If you're feeling low, immersing yourself in the world of everyone's achievements and travel and charity work and parties and children will amplify your feelings of isolation. It's called "FOMO," the fear of missing out.
- You'll find it impossible to resist checking in on old girl/boyfriends. Do not search for exes unless you are feeling 100 percent confident in your life. Set an egg timer and stop after three hours.
- Privacy settings are also changing constantly. If you are not a teenager, make friends with one who will correctly toggle the right buttons to keep you safe from Facebook predators.
- Keep it short and sweet: Save details for your real friends.

Someone Is Watching You Read This Right Now

As they used to say when I was a kid, *you're on Candid Camera*! Skype and Facetime allow you to create a live feed from almost any location to any location. We've become comfortable posing for a camera, even a hidden one. These video-chat features on small handhelds will become increasingly pervasive, and with that, say goodbye to your last vestige of privacy.

My youngest daughter began using Skype on her computer, which sits in a hallway nook. I quickly realized whomever she's Skyping has a little window into our world. This terrifying idea has me editing my behavior. No longer can I stroll through the house half-dressed or bark orders at the family without becoming self-conscious of possible surveillance.

In other words, if you've got kids, your entire life is now up for pop inspection. With this in mind, your only choice is to adopt business-professional protocols in your own home. (Time to build that panic room, so you'll have a place to panic in privacy!) And do remind yourself and your kids that all the rules of phone etiquette apply here in double-doses—no eating or other distracting behaviors. Plus, this technology potentially makes sexting look tame. Keep an eye on those kids!

Bonus Tip

Spoiler alert! If you are going to post about a television show's plot developments or live-blog an awards show, please take care to mark your tweets with a spoiler alert or let readers know you're posting results as they come in. It's become an online convention with the serialized nature of shows that everyone seems to care about.

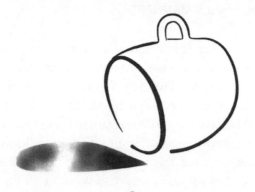

4

Step Into My Office

Understand this, and you will understand everything about this town: A pro never punches out. Whether it's a charity fundraiser, a movie premiere, or your kid's soccer game, you need to be *on*—you're at work, not at play. This is a dog-eat-dog town and everyone you meet is part of the food chain. Lawyers, agents, graphic designers, stylists, gaffers, sound engineers, development girls, photographers, assistants, marketing people, journalists, mailroom boys, and talent . . . there are very few civilians here. Even during a trip to the local watering hole, whether that's Porta Via on Canon or some late-night dive bar in Hollywood, the other jungle animals are watching each other—and *you*.

There's no dividing line between working and socializing here.

I know. The rules don't seem to apply to the "thin air" crowd—the ones who give orders, not take them. Absolute power, yadda yadda. This town runs on that maxim. For some, status seems to equal a blank check drawn from the bank of bad behaviors. You'll recognize them from the atrocities spewed at cowering underlings as they bulldoze through life, equating their success with authority. How dreary.

For the rest of us, however, who work in traditional environs or aspire to a more civilized way of conducting business, there is a laundry list of protocols we must develop to avoid spinning down the road of scandal, disgrace, or humiliation, as fun and attractive as that sounds! In this ferociously competitive, global business environment, everything matters and no one can afford even the slightest misstep.

Don't wait for a call from Human Resources to find out where you went wrong.

And yes, those at the top might one day go off the rails and wish they'd been more aware of those little business etiquette checks and balances that keep the wheels of industry turning smoothly. Civilians know this, and even our intelligence community understands the benefits.

The most fascinating inquiry I've received by far was from an intelligence officer for a nearby armed forces base. She was interested in a program for a group of officers who had recently been released and required skills to integrate back into their home lives. They were so accustomed to interrogating suspicious persons that when it came time to return to their families, they were inadvertently interrogating them and making it miserable for everyone. Additionally, the young male soldiers

*were not making wise choices when it came to their con-
duct after hours, especially in foreign territories where
they behaved like wild teenagers. I proposed a thorough
program working through the differences between business protocols on the job and social courtesies at home.
The hope was that the officers would regard these skills
as invaluable as some of the other covert training they
had received.*

You Got the Interview. Now What?

A lot of people in this town seem to "fail upward"—they crash
and burn at job after job and yet keep riding the invisible
escalator to higher-paying positions with better benefits and
groovier perks. It's clear that employers don't rely on refer-
ences from previous places of employment. This phenomenon
may arise from the understanding that the entertainment biz is a
non-stop clash of egos and personalities—"creative differences"
as the phrase goes.

Most job descriptions in this industry are amorphous (and amphibious).

Since positions are not based on skills, but personality,
your job interview is your best opportunity to make a good
impression. And by "good impression," I mean not be *annoying*. Don't fidget, whine, or waste anyone's time by turning
"ummmmmm" into a background noise. Traits employers
are looking for in this town? Be easygoing, unimpressed,
unflappable. If some A-list person calls, stammering is not
an option. It also helps if you're totally connected in some
youthsphere demographic your potential employer aspires
to reach.

Long before the interview is conducted, prospective employees should also scour their social media for any red flags. Anything that defames your image should be wiped clean. A reminder of the basics:

- Dress for interview success. Go classic, but don't be afraid to show a little style.
- Arrive on time or even early. Five to ten minutes in advance is perfect.
- Turn off electronic devices or leave your phone in the car.
- Make a positive first impression. Remember, no second chances.
- Know how to properly shake hands. Don't make them do a double-take with a limp handshake.
- Notice body language. Open body position, with nothing crossed, is best.
- Perfect your conversation skills. Avoid one-word answers.
- Prepare a list of intelligent questions. Refrain from reiterating the obvious.
- Practice graceful goodbyes. Exit as elegantly as you arrived.
- Write a thank-you note. Most people do not do this, so you are guaranteed to stand out!

Separate Yourself from the Pack

I'm always surprised that business people seldom utilize thank-you notes. Whether you are following up on an introduction, interview, or meeting, nothing conveys your appreciation better. Since so few of us take the time, this daring act differentiates you from all the sloths who don't spend the extra six minutes. And yes, you can send an email, especially if you're addressing an ecotist or a technobrat.

If someone's really worked overtime for you, please do send a gift. Order flowers, send a trendy plant, or hit a cute gift store. Personalize as needed.

Suit Up

One little shocker about this town—the rattier you dress, the more likely people will think you're *talent*. And *talent* is king ("talent" referring *not* to the acting gifts, but to the actual actors). These would be the ones who believe dressing down makes them incognito—like anybody is fooled by a famous face dressed as a truck driver, waiting for a seat at a $300-tab sushi bar.

The bright young things have picked up on the phenomenon and used this reverse psychology to obtain certain local perks—tables at hot restaurants, entry past velvet ropes at underground bars—all the while contributing to the increasing plague of casual-wear. Yes, track pants, ripped jeans, flip-flops, hoodies. Please don't make me continue.

> *This is the only place in the world where dressing like an ex-con will not get you followed around by security at a fancy department store.*

Second, this place is freebie central—free shirts, face creams, movie screeners, cameras, sneakers, jewelry, whatever. Everyone works in the industry or knows someone who does, so every day of the week brings a fresh round of offerings from hopeful vendors. Armies of swag-bags block your exit from each and every Beverly Hills event, charitable or otherwise. No one knows how to go to an actual clothing store and assemble an outfit. Instead, it's *this* band t-shirt, with *these* gratis jeans and *those* weird one-off sneakers from the Grammy party . . . get the picture?

On the other hand, agents—those who work at entertainment talent agencies—seem to negotiate deep discounts at high-end stores (in return for what, I do not wish to know). This professional class is expected to own a walk-in closet filled with expensive suits, even if one occupies a lowly post in the mailroom. ("It's temporary, *I'm on my way up!*")

While we're on the subject of agents (whom I love, I might add—they make the world go round in these parts), the Ari Gold character on television's *Entourage* isn't a figment of imagination. He exists, here, in both the male and female form. Agents who serve the A-list need to have egos equal to their clients. But that vibe doesn't jive for those who aren't at the tippy top.

I was approached by an agent with a bad reputation. He needed what we call a page-one rewrite, referring to a script-writer's worst nightmare: a top-to-bottom makeover. This is a great place to start: a client who realizes his or her mistakes are holding back a bright career, and is willing to do the work to fix the problems. We jumped right in with an overall attitude adjustment toward showing appreciation, gratitude, and mutual respect with his clients and coworkers, pointing out the small courtesies and larger gestures that work wonders. The result, career longevity.

In other words, the help is expected to wear a crisp, freshly pressed uniform.

And now you're beginning to grasp the social structure of this town.

Of course, as a sensible, responsible person, I reject this entire dynamic. Unless you are a youthful billionaire, e.g., you are the real Mark Zuckerberg, you do not have the luxury of looking like a shlub. With dozens of paparazzi hanging out on every corner, all dangling telephoto lenses the length of elephant trunks, even the young and beautiful must reconsider their lax attitude ("laxitude"?) on style.

The interweb is plastered with pictures of hapless celebrities, caught offguard in outfits best described as "unfortunate."

I would remind you—again—that there are no private moments in this town, and you need to look your best—especially in a professional situation. Whatever your work, you want to be taken seriously. You will not be taken seriously in business if you're dressed for a luau, a strip club, or a rodeo—unless you live in Hawaii, are a stripper or a cowboy, or are on your way to audition for a role playing a hula dancer, stripper, or cowboy.

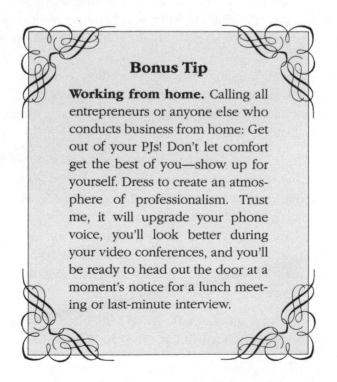

Bonus Tip

Working from home. Calling all entrepreneurs or anyone else who conducts business from home: Get out of your PJs! Don't let comfort get the best of you—show up for yourself. Dress to create an atmosphere of professionalism. Trust me, it will upgrade your phone voice, you'll look better during your video conferences, and you'll be ready to head out the door at a moment's notice for a lunch meeting or last-minute interview.

If you work in an office, you will invest in the following colors: beige, navy, charcoal gray, white, ivory, and black, all expressed in quality fabrics. You will decorate your body with smart accessories: a timepiece, stylish shoes, elegant jewelry, tasteful scarves and ties. You will adorn classic lines that fit instead of pinch or sag, cinch or cut. You will dry clean these items on a regular basis at the green dry cleaner. And if this sounds like conformity, that's because it *is*, and you *will*. Conform. Because that's what *paycheck* means. Fun!

Hug It Out or Just Shake Hands?

We have already covered the successful handshake in full. With that in mind, whether you're in the boardroom or at a poolside mixer with your colleagues, keep your right hand free (and dry). You'll get flustered juggling that cold, wet drinking glass from right to left if a VIP (future spouse, A-list client) turns a corner—and worse, you'll *look* flummoxed, too.

In general, hugging between coworkers is not standard across industry, with some exceptions—any industry based in ancient Italian protocols, for example (fashion, design, the music industry, crime).

> The Today Show *asked me to do a piece on the "man hug" when President Obama first took office in 2009— that simultaneous handshake/pat on the shoulder move introduced to break down racial barriers and party lines and usher in a more inclusive and welcoming era. The President's man-hug successfully conveyed that extra bit of warmth our country was looking for at the time.*

The twenty-somethings are far less inhibited in the workplace than the fifty-somethings. The "hipster" industries are more responsive to such contact than, say, the indifferent, blue-chip corporate cultures.

> *Hold off while you observe corporate culture*
> *before tackling your colleagues, however warmly.*

Don't forget the universal rules of body language, which apply to every generation, every situation. Be direct with your eye contact. Don't hesitate, because you'll look like you're hiding something. Darting eyes, hands hidden in pockets, crossed arms, and general fidgeting will put everyone within a six-foot radius in attack mode. Let's agree we don't want that.

In short, be at ease to put others at ease.

Age Before Beauty (There Is an Established Hierarchy)

Yes, please, *stand* for all business introductions, say your first and last name, as well as the name of your company. Always respond to an introduction using the most respectful and deferential manner. And observe the hierarchy (even if you find that notion a tad insulting), top to bottom. You know from watching *Mad Men* that the client always comes first.

Note to the entire cast: Stay on script for all business introductions. This is no place to improvise, try out a new comedy sketch, or inject unwanted drama.

Your line: "It's nice to meet you."

Or, if it feels real: "It's a pleasure to meet you."

Make sure you haven't already met. If in doubt, utilize the old reliable backside-cover: "It's nice to *see* you."

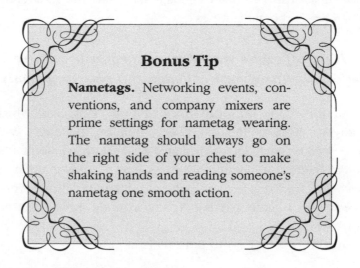

Bonus Tip

Nametags. Networking events, conventions, and company mixers are prime settings for nametag wearing. The nametag should always go on the right side of your chest to make shaking hands and reading someone's nametag one smooth action.

Get Actual Business Cards

Has the traditional business card gone the way of landlines and holiday cards? I hope not. A beautifully designed card printed on a letterpress on heavy cardstock makes a far better introduction than a smartphone bump. Note to those fresh out of college: The old men are still running the show. And most of them don't know the difference between a tweet and an Angry Bird. Print up a set of cards unless you want to live above your parents' garage for the rest of your life. Here are the ingredients for a successful paper-based introduction:

- A card makes an **effective tool** that will help your business contacts remember you.
- A card **brands** your company and your corporate culture in the moment. What's the chance they'll really take the time to visit your web site?
- It will **impress** your father, who doesn't think you have a "real" job.

- Always have your cards **on hand**, in sufficient quantity, in a fancy sleeve or case so they don't get stained or dog-eared.
- When presented with a card, take a moment to review it, possibly pay a compliment on the design, and then place it carefully on your person. In other words, **don't stash it in your jeans** with your keys and lint.
- If you want to give someone a card, **ask** for his or hers.
- Beware of offering a card **too soon**. Your enthusiasm may come across as pushy. Wait for the opportune time to present.
- Stay current on adding contacts electronically, but **keep cards** in case of the inevitable hard drive crash or stolen phone.

Leave It at Home: Personal Business at Work

I've been forging my way as my own boss for more than ten years, but in the past I really enjoyed working in offices. My first job, as an assistant in the international department of a major record label, was incredibly exciting. I had the time of my life meeting artists, attending concerts, and listening to great music. I enjoyed dressing for work and interacting with my co-workers. I loved the sense of accomplishment I felt at the end of the day.

Still, we've all had tough jobs, working for cruel, exacting, unfair people. And there are a lot of books (and lawyers) that specialize in dealing with such unpleasant scenarios.

The less you reveal about your personal life at work, the better. Apart from the cold, hard fact that no one is interested, understand that such information will invariably be used against you. Sure, right now everyone's telling you that the company is like one, big, happy family. Have you ever spent any time in a family? Then you know that nothing is forgotten, no matter how long ago or how particularly damaging or incriminating or embarrassing the information. The less of your personal life you allow to bleed into the workplace, the better. Same goes for family.

There is no personal business at work.

Answer calls and read emails and texts on *your* cellular device on *your* breaks. Never utilize work email for personal business. Not only are your corporate overlords collecting those emails, but they're also keeping them. Forever. They own them. Do not let them own you. Got it?

There is no play at work. You are getting paid to work, not conduct your social life—unless socializing is actually your job, and then it better say so somewhere in your title and job description. It doesn't? I didn't think so. Any behavior of this kind that gets noticed will count against you at promotion time.

There is no personal space at work. However, there are distinct boundaries. Knock *verbally* when walking into someone's open office, especially if they are focused on work. Step into their line of vision so they don't have to scan the entire room to find you.

> *There is no attitude at work. I had to conduct a seminar at a medical practice because somehow the receptionists had the idea that snippy and rude behavior helps ease the nervousness of patients visiting the doctor. I'm sure they also had no idea that their jobs were dependent on how well they listened to my advice.*

Go Pro

You're out of your league and loving it, in a room full of hardened business professionals in an industry you've been dreaming about since you were a kid. How do you fit in? How do you stand out without *standing out?* Simple answer: Make like a smoothie and blend in. Begin your new job by observing the corporate (or non-corporate) culture—listening more than talking and showing respect for those wearing the stripes. Hold off on sharing your unique perspective until you are 100 percent sure of where you are and who you are with. Most likely, that will be never.

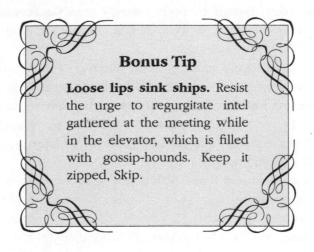

Bonus Tip

Loose lips sink ships. Resist the urge to regurgitate intel gathered at the meeting while in the elevator, which is filled with gossip-hounds. Keep it zipped, Skip.

The more you practice professional etiquette at work, the less you'll be drawn into conflict quicksand.

In broad terms, etiquette is about quashing ego by drawing attention away from oneself. We are tempted to engage with work on an emotional level, but maintaining distinct professional formality and objectivity at work will always pay off. Conflicts are inevitable, especially when egos are on parade, in full costume, and armed with megaphones, as they are in this town. The less personal you make work, the less your own ego will be on the line. This is the highest practice of etiquette. If others freak out on you, who cares? It's not about you; it's about them. Don't take it personally if your fellow employees hang their issues out to dry.

Repeat after me: It's just business.

- **Don't confuse your job with your life.** Don't bring it home. And don't bring your life to work. Keep it separate.
- **Put 100 percent of your energy into performance.** Develop impeccable work habits. Arrive on time, stay focused while on the job.
- **Blend in.** Don't stand out and don't grab the spotlight. Because we dislike people who do that, with a vengeance.
- **Support and encourage others with positive energy.** Avoid negative statements at all costs. Because everything you say is being recorded, by all ears, for later playback at the water cooler.
- **Keep detached from office politics.** View work as a vacation break from your tumultuous personal life, not the other way around.
- **Refuse the rabble-rousers.** Politely display your compassion for their issues and return to work.
- **Steer clear from taking sides in conflicts.** Especially if you're new. You don't know the history or who is wearing the white hats. Bad guys are more likely to try to recruit you into their dead-end conflicts than good guys.
- **Don't be available 24-7.** Establish your boundaries from day one.
- **Crying in the workplace.** Refrain from crying in the workplace, period. Restrict the drama for the big screen where at least you stand a chance to win an award for your efforts.

Bonus Tip

Save, don't send. If you have a brilliant idea after hours, go ahead and compose your thought in an email, but heaven forbid, don't send it! Late-night communications often get overlooked. Also, late-night thoughts can be over-enthusiastic and under-thought. And never put anything negative or inappropriate or damaging to another employee in writing. Put your message in draft form, check through a couple of times the following morning, then hit the send button. Getting in the habit of composing without filling in the addressees is also a useful failsafe.

There Will Be Meetings

And you'll want to give your full attention to whoever is conducting the meeting and anyone who speaks during the meeting. Understand that everyone in the meeting would rather be somewhere else, chewing on a croissant or sneaking a smoke or texting a hot prospect.

You are not the only one tempted to play with your laptop, tablet, or smartphone.

To the extent that you can fight the temptation to play with one of these electronic toys, you will display your devotion to professionalism and good manners. Because even if the meeting is boring you—which it is—if you look bored, you will be noticed and it will be noted. And remember, there are as many equally unfulfilling jobs offered by the fast food industry. You do not want to find out firsthand.

Answer the Phone!

What businesslike phone demeanor sounds like: professional and pleasing. Your tone should be amiable and your pronunciation clear and audible. Avoid squawking, shrieking, lingering, chewing, or barking. You are not a terrier, although sometimes you do a great imitation of one. Here are the basics:

- **Placing a call.** Always identify yourself along with your company name and the location, if applicable.
- **Use formal titles.** Titles of address and other signs of deference display the utmost professionalism. Be sure to give clear information, including your name, company, location, telephone number, and the purpose of your call.
- **Receiving a call.** Use a pleasant greeting and convey relevant information. "Good morning (afternoon, evening), Highly Professional Productions, this is Adam Brighteyes speaking, how may I assist you?"
- **Returning calls.** This should occur within a twenty-four-hour period if possible. If your party is unavailable, leave a succinct message including your name, title, company, telephone number, and the purpose of your call.
- **Rolling calls.** The entertainment industry is famous for lobbing calls at the perfect, inappropriate time when they know the recipient is unavailable, at lunch, or has left the building, simply so that they can say they left a message and throw the ball in the other court. Oh please, dispose of this bad habit; it's so junior varsity.

- **Your recorded message.** Post-college, there is no excuse for the personalized message on your cell phone to be set to your favorite retro eighties song. Record a generic, succinct message for your callers; do not hold callers hostage while waiting for the blessed beep.

Everyone Looks Like Hell on Skype

Popular misconception: Skype, Facetime, and other such video-conferencing technologies somehow provide a barrier between participants that allows you to answer email, play a video game on a handheld, or not wear pants—unfortunately, just the look on your face will give you away. Worse, the webcam quality will likely make your skin look like crumpled wax paper. In other words, you're competing with the worst mug shot ever displayed on TMZ. Also, all your fidgeting will be framed and amplified.

Avoid these simple mistakes with a thoughtful set-up:

- Schedule video calls in advance with all parties, and even for one-on-one conferences.
- Make sure everyone is on the same page by establishing an agenda ahead of time to keep this session as quick and productive as possible.
- Preselect a facilitator who will take responsibility for introductions and run the meeting.
- Test before your conference. A quick microphone, speaker, and lighting (and makeup!) check will help you be seen and heard with the best quality.
- Establish good posture relative to your webcam.
- Dress properly as you would for any business meeting—stay away from bright colors and stripes, which are particularly distracting on video. Avoid dangling, jangly jewelry. You'll be tempted to play with it.

- Mute your cell phone, landline, and other devices that might interrupt your conference.
- Ask permission if you wish to record a video conference. Consent must be given.

During the Video Conference:

- Properly introduce yourself and the others in attendance.
- Don't interrupt or speak over people—especially when on a multi-party video conference—it's actually worse than in person!
- Avoid side conversations. It amplifies the chaos.
- Take this opportunity to observe others' body language, as education toward what works and what doesn't in this setting.
- Facial expressions are read loud and clear on video, just as they are in person, so remain conscious and send the right message.
- Be mindful of background noise, doors slamming, or shouting in the other room.
- Speak clearly and slowly, as computer microphones don't always do the human voice justice.
- Oh goodness, do not eat your lunch during this session.
- Be mindful of the cultural dos and don'ts when videoconferencing with clients and colleagues around the globe; you want to be careful not to offend.

Power Dinnering

Contrary to the popular belief that no one in the greater Los Angeles area ever allows foodstuff to enter his or her gastrointestinal system, please join me on a stroll through Beverly Hills at any mealtime. You will see everyone in town, chatting at café tables and stuffing food in their faces—brioche breakfast at Bouchon, chicken hash at the Grill, or bites of Branzino at E. Baldi.

But believe me, between bites, it's all business, whether it's a mea culpa between studio heads, a last-ditch effort from a star in need of a new TV series deal, or a million-dollar marketing effort for an upcoming motion picture franchise. Americans are catching up to the international community, breaking bread over business. And we have some brushing up to do, in terms of our comfort level with this activity. A few tips:

- **Scout the spot.** You should always maintain a home-away-from-home at several local restaurants of varying formality. Build a relationship with the staff, from the owner to the pot-scrubbers. You'll be at ease, get a great table, and be treated like a king whenever you arrive. Your guests will think the world loves you. But—don't make your guest travel across the entire LA basin to get to you.

- **Make reservations.** When you make the invitation, you'll be making the reservation and paying the bill, although you need to offer a choice of restaurants to your guest. In business, avoid any place that doesn't take reservations, because you don't want to negotiate a deal while waiting in an hour-long line for your bagel and lox at Nate 'N Al's. Reconfirm reservation and guests the day before. This town is known for double and sometimes triple-booking meals, so you must never assume.

- **Arrive early to set the stage.** Make sure the table you want is still available and chat with the servers. One trick is to give the cashier your credit card in advance so there's no awkward tug-of-war over the bill. Your guest can be ten minutes late before you decide he's rude. With the crazy traffic in this town, there's little you can do.

- **Seat your guest.** If the maitre d' is leading, let your guest walk ahead of you so he or she may be seated first. If it's "seat yourself," take the lead. Offer the "power" seat to your guest—the seat that faces the best view.

- **Treat waitstaff like royalty.** It's a real test of character and the best people accord waiters all the respect in the world. They are serving you food. Get it? Also, the single most unattractive trait on the planet is to use your (brief) position of power as a customer to be cruel to others.

- **Observe mobile phone etiquette.** Keep phones off the table, and if you are expecting a wildly urgent call, warn your guest in advance and take the call away from the table.

- **Ordering your meal.** Don't dither, because you want to get to business as quickly as possible. Avoid messy plates in business. It's hard to be taken seriously if you're wearing a bib, or worse, a large hunk of lasagna on your lapel. Also, if you order first, you're setting the price window for your guests, so let them order first. This is a good place to establish that you're hosting. And please don't get weird with your sugar-free, gluten-free, white-meat-only threats that make others uncomfortable.

- **The boarding house reach.** Whatever you grab for on the table—bread, butter, ketchup, whatever—offer it to your guests first.

- **Drinking.** Breakfast or lunch, you won't be ordering a drink. Not in this town. Not in this country. Not since the economic crash. At dinner, it's acceptable, but limit your intake to two or fewer drinks (loose lips, et cetera). If you don't drink, you don't have to broadcast it, just order a non-alcoholic beverage in a highball.

- **Smoking.** Nicotine mints were invented so you don't leave your guest twiddling with his smartphone while you share a smoke in the alley with the cooking staff.

- **Hold off on business during the meal.** Wait until the meal is finished before initiating any serious talk about business. Documents may be placed on the table toward the end of the meal, but keep briefcases tucked under. If you need to use your laptop or tablet, move closer to your guest so you can view the screen together more easily.

- **Tip your waiter.** Twenty percent. Don't cheat your server in front of a potential business partner. Bad form. He'll assume correctly you plan to shortchange him, too.
- **Make a clean exit.** When your guest is ready, leave the restaurant together. Repeat the handshake protocols.
- **Follow up.** Email at the end of the day, or if appropriate, write a thank-you note on company letterhead, reaffirming your future business relationship.

Global Economy 101

God bless Americans and our overriding belief that this is the only country in the world. For example, some of us seem to really believe Canada is a nation of troubled comedians. And Mexico? Apparently comprised entirely of friendly gardeners. Hey folks, Canada and Mexico are right next door! Imagine what happens when people from far-flung lands come here to do business.

A meeting can quickly turn into a bad manners free-for-all, where a few simple gestures can offend a visiting dignitary and kill a deal cold. Outside of the United States, formality is not about wealth, it's about respect. Sure, we're about moxie, verve, and spontaneous energy, like a messy, precocious kid who thinks everyone loves him. Elsewhere in the world, tradition is to be observed and preserved. Luckily for us, most international travelers already expect us to be ruder than children.

*Here's a switch: Let's surprise the visitors to
our country with our good manners!*

Before conducting business with individuals from other
countries, please educate yourself a bit. Working from an
awareness of subtle language and cultural differences in
business transactions is a million times smarter than smash-
ing your way through, believing your winning personality is
all you need to succeed. Whatever your business partners
think of you, they'll think of all Americans, so regard yourself as a diplomat.

> *This can get especially tricky at the corporate
> level. Companies have a limited ability to instill
> rules and enforce them in this age of litigation.
> So they often hire consultants, such as myself,
> to gently intercede. I was contacted by a local
> five-star hotel interested in training their staff
> on how to interact with international guests.
> I spent two days working with the employees of
> each department on cultural sensitivities, intro-
> ducing dignitaries, and keeping professional
> distance while building customer relationships.*

Do the homework:

- Teach yourself a few key words and phrases from their
  native language (don't expect to use them, just know
  them).
- Learn a few facts about their culture and customs.
- Educate yourself on their cuisine and dietary restrictions.
- Err on the side of formality—casual dress does not exist
  and business executives are always addressed by their
  titles and full name, not by first names.

- Note dining rules—for example, in their native countries, Indians and Moroccans eat with their hands.

> *I once worked with an Asian executive who was having difficulty conveying the notion of dress codes to his staff. It may be perfectly acceptable to wear low-cut tops and high-cut skirts at a motorcycle trade show in, say, Nowwheresville, but not a corporate business conference in Hong Kong. And yes, he was grappling with one employee in particular, who was otherwise a very valuable asset to the company. To avoid singling her out, I suggested an international image/grooming/attire workshop for the entire group.*

Outtake

A Quick Trip Around the World of Business Protocols

Japan

- In Japan, the customs are so strict that a simple, innocent mistake can cost you the deal.
- Most Japanese businesspeople shake hands and bow when greeting. The degree of the bow is as important as the action. The deeper the bow, the more respect you show.
- Handshake is a light grip, three or four gentle pumps. It is best to avoid any physical contact except a handshake.
- Exchanging of business cards involves specific protocols and is done so with reverence. Present the card using both hands while bowing slightly. Your fingers should not cover your name, company name, or logo. View the card

thoroughly. The longer you look at the card, the more respect you are showing the person. Never put the card away immediately. Be prepared to carry a large quantity of business cards as the Japanese are fond of exchanging them.

- Gift-giving in Japan is deeply rooted in Japanese culture. Always bring gifts for new and old contacts. Stay away from gifts displaying company logos. Wrappings should be natural paper or colorful fabric squares and no ribbons. Presenting your gift properly is expected. As with business cards, gifts are offered with both hands.

Europe

- Business card protocol is a bit more relaxed and involves little ceremony.
- Business cards are exchanged frequently and typically at the onset of a meeting, so carry a large supply.
- A handshake is a quick grasp and then release. An exception is the United Kingdom, where an initial handshake may be the only one you receive.
- Business gifts across most of Europe should not be too personal and should always be wrapped meticulously.

Middle East

- Titles of address in the Middle East are important.
- Expect to exchange business cards with everyone.
- Always present and receive business cards with two hands, facing the person to whom you're giving a card, and make a point of studying the card before putting it into a business card holder.
- Gift giving is common in Middle Eastern cultures.
- Acceptable gifts are high-quality office accessories or items of silver, porcelain, and crystal.

- Crossing your legs and showing the soles of your shoes or feet is considered incredibly rude.

India

- In general, Indians are formal on the first meeting.
- Elders are respected and deferred to in many situations.
- Handshakes are the norm for most cosmopolitan areas, or you can use the Hindi greeting by holding your palms together in front of your chest and saying, "Namaste."
- Gifts are presented with both hands. Red, green, and yellow are lucky colors and good for gift-wrapping.
- Never point your feet at a person. Feet are considered unclean.
- Business cards are presented with the right hand. Do not use both hands.

Latin America

- Latin Americans are generally very friendly, very physical, and very good hosts.
- Normally, people get to know one another first and then do business.
- Handshakes are firm and relatively brief.
- After a relationship has been established, don't be surprised if you are met with a hug.
- Business cards are exchanged without much ceremony. Just make sure to read it thoroughly once it has been presented to you.
- Gifts in most Latin American countries aren't expected at the first visit; however, gift-giving is more acceptable with subsequent visits.
- Appropriate gifts include fine chocolates, a bottle of wine, or liquor.

5

On Location

The workweek has ended. Finally. Let's go grab a couple sparkling watermelon martinis, maybe swing by the Polo Lounge. Time to cut loose, hit a few crowded watering holes, ogle some cute assistant-types, knock back one too many, vent your righteous frustrations, get into an altercation with a bitter out-of-work actor, and maybe break something expensive. For the next forty-eight hours, it's all about you. Right?

No, dear.

To repeat: A pro never punches out.

Not in this town. Everyone's a pro here, of some sort. Everyone is always working—working *it*. You don't advance your career at work; here, you advance your career when you're out, being there and doing that. In marketing terms, we call this "raising brand awareness."

First of All, You'll Need a Date

Let's go over a couple details about dating in Beverly Hills. Forget everything you've ever learned about love in less professional climates. You've stepped into a vast arena where career is everything, and your heart better have the cold, hard detachment and fortitude of a gladiator. Because in this town, a date is part trendy accessory and part vehicle for advancement. Your choice of companion will be seen as an expression of your business prowess and your status on the food chain—an extension of your precious brand. In other words, the factors you will consider in dating someone will be the same as buying a car: looks, reliability, and price.

In more normal centers of human interaction, the story is always the same. Boy meets girl (nouns interchangeable), boy and girl get together for no good reason, maybe get married, have some babies, eventually end up hating each other. It will be a character-driven story, featuring true love and other insanities: a tearjerker, full of plot twists and heartbreak.

Here, stories of relationships resemble an annual report; a corporate merger featuring announcements of strategic partnerships, rising stock, and horizontal (vertical, et al.) integration.

Meanwhile, dating protocols are driven by digital immediacy. Courtship? Gone are the days of setting up a date a week in advance at some fine dining establishment where every detail would be choreographed ahead of time. Invitations come as texts, loose recommendations to meet up, hook up, and/or break up, at some LinkedIn event. You don't really need to interrogate your date because you've already Googled her/his name, ten pages deep. In fact, you probably met through one of those myriad online dating services and studied his/her profile assiduously. When I was a youngster, a dating service meant desperation. Now it's accepted methodology, a means to access an unbelievable quantity of potential. And with that buffet of possibilities, we can sample everything in a relatively short amount of time. Didn't love it? Try something else.

Personally, I believe that people never change. We're all secretly looking for those deep, spiritual unions that last a lifetime.

Best of luck.

Revive Chivalry

Let's step into the past for a moment, when chivalry was part of the courtship canon: guidelines men observed as custom when accompanying a lady out and about. These days, women need to adopt the same attitude toward gracious behavior as the gentlemen of the past did. More and more, responsibility is falling on young women to step into society as alphas, taking care of elderly parents and the like, even as some ladies take on the role of gentlemen in dating situations. Let's add the word "lady" to the following set of traditional protocols to ensure that chivalry is universal, across gender.

A gentleman/lady shows consideration wherever he/she goes by:

- Applying the words "please" and "thank you" liberally.
- Displaying respect toward everyone, equally.
- Observing agreed-upon schedules with precise punctuality.
- Refraining from texting and taking or making phone calls while in the company of others.
- Holding doors open for anyone coming through, carrying heavy packages, and assisting a companion with putting on a coat. Picking up and returning any item another person has accidently dropped (including hints).
- Taking the curbside position while walking together down the street to protect a companion's clothing from wet gutter mud splattering from a passing car.

- Allowing one's companion to choose a seat at a restaurant and pulling out the chair to seat that companion.
- Standing up when one's companion leaves a table or returns.
- Once upon a time, a gentleman would always wait for a lady to initiate a handshake because he should never *presume* that a lady would wish to make any kind of physical contact. Figure this one out for yourself with respect to gender roles.
- When inviting a companion to dinner, traditional roles would dictate that a gentleman always offers to pay because money is never a consideration. If your companion insists on either paying ("I'd really like to pick this up, would you mind?) or sharing the bill, you will always defer to the companion's wishes.
- He/she is equally gracious and polite when speaking to the wait staff at the restaurant. He/she is invested in the overall experience rather than scrutinizing each detail of the check with a fine-tooth comb. Because that is so %$#@! annoying.
- He/she maintains excellent eye contact throughout the conversation, making his/her dining companions feel like they are the only people in the room.
- He/she maintains a positive attitude and exudes a natural sense of cool and control. He/she possesses a distinct allure that makes him/her at once electrifying to be around and yet secure and comforting.

The older you get, the harder it is to transform. I once received a call from the president of a sorority at a well-known Los Angeles university. An emergency intervention was required for the young men taking up residence in the neighboring fraternity. Potty mouths, repulsive humor,

*slovenly hygiene, and lack of respect toward the
ladies had amplified their bad habits to epic
proportions. I was pretty certain my program
would be met with resistance, and possibly rot-
ten fruit. So I dressed to the nines, figuring a
spoonful of sugar might help the medicine go
down easier. The guys were completely unpre-
pared for my message, namely that the behaviors championed in the frat house would come
back and haunt them later. I introduced them
to the concept of chivalry. No stone was left
unturned; surprisingly, shockingly, they actually enjoyed the show.*

Outtake

Dating in the Digital Age

Please remember that your date is a person, not a statistic.
Yes, there is a cornucopia of choices nowadays. But never
ever treat anyone as if he or she is a commodity in a supply-
and-demand curve. We all become very sensitive when we
think we're being viewed as an object. You may be in last-
ditch desperation (to erase the memory of your previous
romantic disaster), but please limit the number of prospects
you are meeting in any one arc so that you can get to know
someone. Otherwise, what's the point?

- **Negotiations.** We all have our own style, but playful
  banter is usually the best ammo when meeting someone
  online. However, sexting before you've met someone is
  not a very splendid idea. What if there's zero chemistry
  when you finally meet face-to-face? *Awkward.*
- **Enticements.** Emailing sexy photos, even after you've met
  someone, is less than prudent. Do you really want to risk

that photo being posted on Facebook if he/she turns out to be a creep? Of course you don't.

- **Clarify goals.** Be clear about your intentions. If you are interested in a casual relationship, make it known. There is no shame in it. But when one person is looking for casual and the other is looking for a life partner, the schism will amplify as you spend more time with each other. Heartbreak!

- **Be gracious.** Always thank your companion for the pleasure of their company, even if the date didn't generate desired fireworks. Regardless of money spent, both of you took time out of your busy lives to invest in a potential connection. Example kiss-off, sent by text/email/Facebook messenger: "Thank you very much for a pleasant evening. I didn't feel any romantic chemistry between us, but I wish you all the best. Thanks again for your time." Let them down easily, spare the tender egos.

- **Don't gossip.** About yourself, or anyone else. Don't talk about exes on a first date . . . just *don't*.

- **Never refer to Googled info.** Of course you Googled his/her name. Just file it as deep background.

- **Attire.** Wear something comfortable for you, but understand that a first date is an experiment in *physical* chemistry, so don't hide yourself in layers of heavy clothing. As with a job interview, overdressing is better than underdressing. You want your date to feel that you are taking meeting him/her seriously.

- **Truth in advertising.** If you need eyeglasses, wear them on the date. The baseball cap won't hide the receding hairline. Hair extensions gone astray may reveal an embarrassing bald spot.

- **Liquor.** Cut yourself off. Everyone should know their limit—don't exceed it. A drink or two may lower a few barriers, but that third one is an unwanted truth serum. Skip it!

- **Strategize.** Don't bare your soul and admit all your faults on a first date. Your date won't either. None of us is perfect, but we don't need to divulge this right away. Best wait until after your wedding day.
- **Be on time.** Don't be late. It's not fashionable.
- **Show consideration.** If you are going to be late, text or call the minute you realize it. Offer to meet another time if timing becomes inconvenient. Explicitly apologize.
- **Muffle distractions.** Set your cell phone to "silent." You could turn it off, as well; however, sometimes on a first date you might want to share something from your smartphone—photos, something from your Facebook profile, etc. And don't noticeably take your cell phone with you to the bathroom. Your date will know you are checking messages and possibly arranging a later hook-up.
- **Focus and be present.** Don't take any notice of the other people at your first date venue, e.g., never, ever flirt with anyone in front of your escort. Treat your companion like he or she is the only person in the room.
- **Don't swoon.** Not yet. Be careful not to be too anxious or adoring. You don't know this person and coming on too strong can be a serious turnoff.
- **Take it to the next level?** If there's chemistry and you feel comfortable, there is no explicit reason you two (three?) shouldn't take it further.
- **Return business.** Never ask for another date during the date if you're a player and want to leverage suspense. If you're not, indicate at the end of the evening that you would like to see your date again; if you ask for another date before the end, it puts your date in an awkward position if he or she would prefer to decline. Also, you don't want to appear overeager. Still, there's no reason to play war games by waiting more than twenty-four hours to schedule another one.

Now Make Your Grand Entrance

What is *It*, exactly? It's what you bring to the party—energy, animation, charisma. It's what makes people think you're rich, powerful, and famous—like everyone else in the room.

You burst through the front door like a gust of warm wind, full of joy, your glowing face saying, "I know, it's me, try to remain calm."

You walk straight and deliberately to the maître d', to the receptionist, to the bouncer—whoever is running the room, whatever room you're walking into—locking eye contact, one pro to another, because you've both done this a million times.

Getting a good table, obtaining intel, moving past the velvet rope . . . it's always about one thing—creating an instant connection by recognizing the professional status of the gatekeeper.

No one likes being invisible, especially those of us in the service industry.

The trick is to award others the power they've earned. Commit the radical act of paying attention to the faceless somebody whom the *amateur* thinks is invisible. The amateur just rushes from one place to the next, completely consumed with his own very special thoughts, never noticing what's going on around him. That's just silly. And it won't get you very far.

Outtake

Hit the Red Carpet Like a Rock Star

Hollywood's famous faces are America's royalty, and the red carpet is like a summons to do tequila shots with the Queen. Red carpet confidence is about exuding the confidence, and yes, *entitlement,* of a superstar. Look the part, feel the part, and let it radiate like Saturday morning sunshine, 150 percent. It's about sporting that *I love you people* smile, despite downpours of self-doubt. It's about projecting energy when you are, in truth, crushed with exhaustion. It's about striving for the upbeat even if you're dragging the world's problems like a lead balloon.

Don't get the wrong idea—I'm not asking you to lie. I'm asking you to allow others to enjoy the moment, to bask in the gala pageant, to soak up a little starry-eyed excitement. Don't rain on their parade from your dark cloud of self-indictments and petty resentments. My God, stop taking yourself so seriously. Take this opportunity to interrupt the litany of self-admonishments. Give yourself the night off.

What does this have to do with me? you ask. You are not a contender for any gold-plated statuettes. You don't even frequent film premieres. Understand: Everyone has a red carpet moment at least once in their lifetime. Instead of succumbing to the fear of not measuring up, make the most of it. One time or another, we all face extremely intimidating gatherings, whether it's the wedding you wish you didn't have to attend, an invitation to a gala out of your social league, or a surprise award for some altruistic act. Who knows? When yours arrives, you will want to act like this level of extravaganza is totally *business as usual* for you. Here's how:

- **Look and feel the part.** Forget this week's trends—wear what best suits your figure and makes you feel most comfortable. Then step it up a notch. Skip risky wardrobe choices that might result in a viral photo of malfunction or unflattering commentary. Go easy on the plunging lines around the décolletage and derrière. Men, do avoid anything that is too tight or *pinchy.*

- **Give it to them straight.** Whatever you do, don't slouch. Good posture not only helps guide you, but also will allow you to move gracefully and effortlessly. Your clothes will also fit better on your body.
- **Flash the cameras your best.** The most slenderizing, attractive pose for a lady is one where her body is turned partially sideways with one shoulder in front of the other. Feet are planted in a model "T" position with the majority of the weight placed on the back foot. Head is forward slightly to reduce a double chin effect. Shoulders are back and stomach is gently held in. Keep your arms loose to prevent any flab-squinching. Finally, both hands on the hips and legs crossed.
- **Keep an air of confidence.** With a warm smile, bright eyes, fresh breath (keep mints handy, lose the chewing gum!), and unselfconscious body movements.
- **Deliver an unforgettable interview.** Be gracious and provide open-ended answers. The words should flow effortlessly and intentionally with perfect diction, grammar, and vocabulary.
- **Own the room.** Stop before entering a room to allow onlookers to notice you. Convince your animal brain that you are top of the food chain and you are advancing on a herd of gazelles. Proceed like you own the scene—not in an arrogant way, but like a lioness surveying her territory with a complete sense of security.
- **Act like the world is your stage.** Make eye contact with people you'd like to meet, and treat them as if you are the only people in the room. Of course, do this without staring and getting confused as a stalker. Never forget: One party can turn your entire life around, 180 degrees, because of someone you might meet there. Make the most of this opportunity.

Bonus Tip

Nominated for an actual award? Prepare your acceptance speech, in writing, and practice it until you have it down cold. Memorize all the names of the people in your category and make sure to acknowledge them along with your other gracious, sincere *thank yous*. That way, your spouse won't have to later remind you of the important names you forgot to mention. Erp.

Even celebs accustomed to the red carpet treatment get the jitters in some places—namely, the red carpet. I worked with an Oscar front runner who was fearing the event. We worked on best poses for photos, calming exercises for increased focus and diction (there was an issue of mumbling), as well as the potential release of foul language, if enthusiasm—not reason—were allowed to guide reactions. Happily, my client ended up taking home the golden statue and hit a home run with the spectators.

Superstar Service

It's insane how you can make a server's day by *not* acting like a demanding, entitled infant. Suddenly, it's all smiles, better service, and free slices of cake. As if by magic, everyone's having a nicer time. It's the little people, the *boors,* who seize these everyday moments of power differences to vocalize their petty authority fantasies, treating us to a bad imitation of middle management. We've all seen it. How *small*.

Here's the logic: The world loves a famous face (no matter whose). When the world loves you, you love it, and everyone in that loving, smiling world loves you back. If you spread love and happiness everywhere you go, it's assumed you're successful, even famous, and unquestionably *alpha*. The luxury of being humble, egalitarian, and sincere marks you as a superstar in this world. The actual superstars will instantly recognize you as one of them. All you're doing is giving someone else a little sunshine.

All you're doing is being *polite*.

Dine with Decorum

You're already bored by the title of this section, but is there anything worse than finding yourself captive at a table while your dinner companion attacks their entrée like a hyena tearing apart road kill? Yes, a couple things come to mind, but let's ignore them for a moment and focus on making the dining experience a universally pleasant one. It is never too late or too early to begin to appreciate the value of table manners. Proper dining skills are essential because many of our most meaningful connections take place around the table—from family fights to business transactions (as well as dinner dates where someone is deciding whether you're the type to take home to meet the parents or discard after the initial thrill has dissipated into a fond memory).

Proficiency in this area eliminates unnecessary distractions so we can enjoy each other's company.

Sit down:

- **Seating arrangements.** The best seat at the table is reserved for the guest of honor or the most senior adult.

On a date, allow your companion to be seated first in the chair with the finest view.

- **Maintain optimum posture.** One cannot possibly enjoy a good meal watching someone slump over the soup. Both feet should be flat on the floor, back straight, shoulders down, and body centered in the chair about three to four inches from the edge of the table.

- **Ordering.** Make friendly eye contact to get your server's attention—a good server will always scan the room to assist a patron in need. If your server is tending to another customer, you may try using the words "excuse me" once he/she breaks away. Know what you would like to order, be concise, and avoid asking unnecessary questions or begging for excessive substitutions to the menu. Remember to use the word "please" when you are placing your order and "thank you" when you are finished.

- **Your place setting is a work of art.** Everything has balance and order. Identify your drinks and bread so you don't accidentally use your neighbors. A little hint I share with my clients, the word *drink* begins with the letters "d-r," which could stand for "drinks right." And on a perfectly balanced table, if the drinks are on the *right*, the bread plate must be on the *left*.

- **Cutlery care.** All utensils are arranged in a specific order, working from the outside going in toward the plate. Forks are on the left with the knives and spoons on the right. The only exception is the butter knife, which may be placed across the bread plate on the left, and the oyster fork, which may be placed on the far right when eating shellfish. When not in use, knives are placed down or inward toward the center of the plate. Once a utensil is dirtied, it never touches the table again. Utensils should not rest halfway on the plate and tablecloth; all oars must be in the boat.

- **Expand your palate.** Your actual palate is located on the roof of your mouth. When someone is said to have a refined palate it means he or she appreciates interesting food. Why yes, you could order the cheeseburger. Again. But you already know what a cheeseburger tastes like. Why not expand your taste horizons when you order out?

When the meal arrives:

- **Wait until everyone has been served.** If you are dining with six people or fewer, it is polite to refrain from eating until everyone has received their food. For larger parties, after five or six people have been served, you may begin eating so that your food does not get cold. When there is a host involved, wait until they invite you to begin.
- **Learn how to eat like the French.** Most Europeans eat Continental style—using their fork with the left hand and the knife in the right. The fork "tines" are aimed face down and used to gently pierce the food while the knife pushes the mushy peas toward the fork. The pattern— cut, then eat, cut, eat—is a much more efficient way than American style (we make things more difficult by add- ing the extra step of placing the knife on the plate and switching hands to bring the food into our mouths right side up) and presents a more polished appearance.
- **Chew with your mouth closed and keep your elbows off the table.** Use Italian hand gestures to communicate until you've fully masticated that mouthful. Forearms are allowed to touch the table between courses or once the ordeal of eating is over.
- **Taste it before seasoning.** Trust the cook, even if you are a saltaholic. If the dish comes up short, then by all means, drown it in salt, pepper, or Sriracha.

- **Divide and conquer the bread.** Bread should be broken into moderate-sized pieces and eaten one bite at a time. It is much nicer looking and saves you the impression that you're trying to shove bread into your mouth.
- **Prevent spills by leaning in over your plate.** Especially soup and other saucy items, none of which would make a good addition to your carefully assembled outfit.
- **If you have to slurp it, skip it.** First impressions are not enhanced by the sight of unsuccessfully navigating foot-long noodles, lobster, chicken on the bone, corn on the cob, some sushi, bouncy little cherry tomatoes, drippy BBQ ribs, and anything that requires a bib.
- **A word about wine.** The "Nectar of the Gods" is meant to be sipped properly. White wine and champagne are both served chilled. Hold these glasses by the stem. Red wine is served room temperature and may be held at the bowl.
- **Remove unwanted items.** The rule of thumb: "Out the way it went in." Find a watermelon seed in your fruit salad? Discard the seed into your spoon. Mouthful of surprise gristle while chewing a piece of steak? Remove with your fingers and deposit it back on the rim of your plate, or your bread plate if it is still visible.
- **Passing items.** Pass plates to the right. Always offer an item to the person on your immediate left first, then help yourself, and continue around the table. Pass all condiments in pairs. "Pass the salt please?" Send around the salt, as well as the pepper.

As we know, money and success don't magically give you sophistication. I've conducted primers in basic table manners in $35 million dollar houses and been paid to school fancy sororities on the proper use of a fork. Poor dining skills *can almost ruin a marriage! A man contacted me in anticipation of an upcoming weekend where his stuffy parents were meeting his thirty-two-year-old fiancé for the first time. The fiancé, a social worker who was not taught proper table manners, was highly offended and hurt over the issue and almost ready to call off the wedding. I sat this woman down and explained that people from all walks of life are challenged at the dinner table. After a few deep breaths, she relaxed, embracing the process, and ultimately enjoyed acquiring the new skills. The groom-to-be, who thought he was just perfect, also learned a thing or two.*

Bonus Tip

Table Napkins

- A napkin is used to wipe food from your mouth, blot your lips before taking a drink, catch crumbs that may fall into your lap, wipe buttery fingertips, or use as a blast-shield if you happen to sneeze or cough while at the table.
- Place napkin on your lap when you sit down and on your chair if you have to step away from the table.
- Place napkin back on the table when you are done.

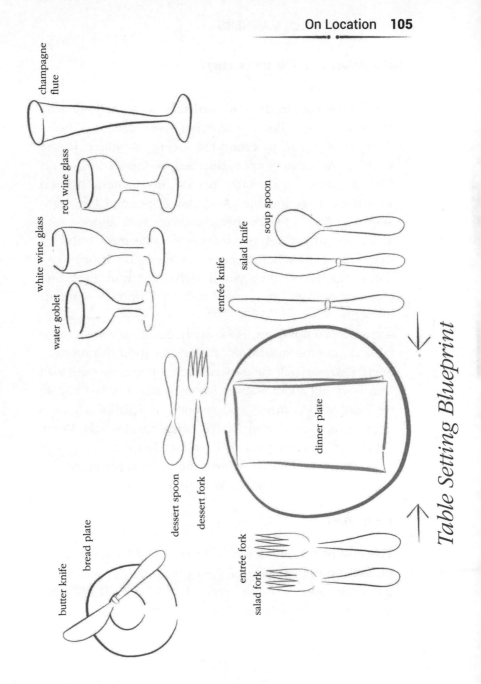

champagne flute

red wine glass

white wine glass

water goblet

soup spoon

salad knife

entrée knife

dessert spoon

dessert fork

dinner plate

butter knife

bread plate

entrée fork

salad fork

Table Setting Blueprint

Make friends with wait staff:

- **Complain sparingly and politely.** If something isn't to your liking, decide whether you ordered incorrectly or if a serious crime has been committed in the kitchen. A sauce you've decided is too rich is your bad; a steak accidentally served raw when ordered well done is actionable. And don't summon the manager if a shred of dark meat has somehow slipped into an entrée advertised as containing white meat only. It's one thing if a kitchen error is impinging on your enjoyment. But remember, you'll definitely ruin everyone else's meal if you get into a battle royale over a minor infraction.
- **Assume the position.** How many times have we left the table during the meal only to find our food has mysteriously disappeared, or experienced an unseasoned wait staff hovering about waiting for us to take our last bite so they can swoop down and remove our plates? There is nothing more frustrating. If eye contact and words do not suffice, try placing your fork and knife on the edges of your plate when taking a break and placing them on the diagonal to the right when you are done.

The big finish:

- **The end of the meal.** Pinch the center of the napkin and place it on the left side of your place setting. When you rise, make sure to return your chair to its original position. Step out into the night air, satisfied.

Bonus Tip

Fast food manners and caffeine fixes. A specific set of manners is required for casual dining and coffee houses. Number one, decide what you are going to order before reaching the front of the line. Two, be quick and courteous when placing your order. Don't stammer and waffle. And I don't care if you feel it's beneath you, learn the café lingo for your order. (Yes, I'm talking about Starbucks; if you want a lot of latté, don't order a "big one," ask for a "venti.") Three, moderate your smash-and-grab attitude toward napkins, condiments, straws, etc. Don't be wasteful. Throw away trash when you are through and leave the table clean for the next customers. Thank you.

Outtake

The Tipping Point

Anyone who's ever had a job in the service industry knows that tipping is an integral part of a service provider's take-home pay. And anyone who's ever been a service provider knows how backbreaking and thankless those jobs are—and tends to leave more than those who have never had to work for a living.

Your command of how much and when to tip will determine whether you will get a fresh cup of coffee or a burned, room-temp cup of vitriol next time you come in. For just a few extra dollars on a lunch bill, on a regular basis, the establishment might be more inclined to squeeze you in on a busy day or bring you a free dessert to try.

> *It's a fairly inexpensive way to show someone you appreciate their effort, as well as contribute to another human's well-being.*

It's expected you will spare 15 percent gratuity for good service and 20 percent or more for exceptional service. Even if you're dissatisfied with your service, it's absolutely unacceptable to skip a tip. Instead, show some bravery and let the staff know if something went wrong (gently). Even in a worst-case scenario—served cat food instead of calamari, leading to a fistfight with the manager—you are still only knocking your gratuity down 10 percent.

A good tip builds relationships, and don't forget to leave extra on holidays and birthdays or other special occasions. If you're a rookie getting some trendy new service (exotic waxing comes to mind), and you don't have a clue what to leave, consult the receptionist for guidance.

Strict Diets Versus Annoyingly Picky Eaters

Beverly Hills is the homeland of trendy diets—the place where all crazy ideas about food originate, then drift out to the rest of mankind. Take a stroll down café row and you'll see the full array of gluten-free, vegan, veggie, dairy-free, anti-candida, raw cuisines. If the diet's hot-off-the-press, severe, and based on some new bizarre research by a pseudo-doctor, someone in this town is using it to carve their backside into perfect, hard marble.

Now I'm all for health and nutrition. Give me fresh pressed juice and a handful of raw toasted almonds any time. Food allergies and even food sensitivities are serious business. But when I'm at a dinner party and someone's got an empty plate because they refuse to consume anything made with milk products, soy, wheat, red meat, or sugar, I have to ask:

Food allergy? Or fad diet so you can fit into your teenaged daughter's jeans?

If it's the latter, which it always is, I refuse to give my blessing. Dining together is an opportunity to forge bonds while breaking bread. If no one's eating bread, forging bonds becomes a little difficult.

If you're on a working health program, there's no reason to choose between your regimen and socializing. Most good hosts usually include lighter or vegetarian choices at their tables. If you're heading to an event that advertises your entire no-fly list, eat beforehand and just refrain from calling attention to your deprivation. The last thing you want to do is bore other guests with your obscure food idiosyncrasies. If it's serious, mention it when you get the invitation.

Bonus Tip

Ignore your neuroses for a night. On a dinner date, particularly a first date, if you submit to the waiter a page-long list of foodstuff you can't eat, please understand your dining companion will bolt when the clock strikes nine. If this is impossible for you, try roller-skating or a trip to the zoo as a first date.

In any case, a good host makes inquiries to see if guests have any severe dietary restrictions.

Taking Tea in Beverly Hills

Thanks to the British mystique—their beautiful accents and skills as storytellers (as I once commented in an article for the *Los Angeles Times* on the Golden Globes, it helps to have a British accent even if you weren't born with one)—Hollywood has always welcomed ex-pats with open arms. Drive through the town and you'll see the influence of generations of homesick Brits, dating back to the 1920s. Among the Spanish revival mansions and mid-century gems clinging to the hills are storybook cottages and Tudor-style mansions, all with perfectly clipped English gardens sporting heirloom roses.

Which brings us to my favorite respite from the crass chaos of our daily scrimmages, a moment of refinement and the height of civility: the British tea ceremony. Afternoon tea is a ritual, an ideal setting for the ultimate test of your etiquette prowess. I've had the pleasure of taking tea and teaching tea at the Peninsula and Montage, two of the city's finest hotels most well-known for their tea service. From the menu of tiny sandwiches to the delicate handling of the teapot, this is a centuries-old tradition. Enjoy!

- **Place settings.** Your teacup is placed on the right side of your place setting. Once a utensil has been used, it stays on the plate.
- **Pinkies.** Raising your pinkie finger is not a pretentious affectation, but rather for better balance to avoid spillage. For best results, pinch the handle of the teacup between the thumb and index finger. Avoid looping fingers through the handle hole or grasping the teacup bowl with both hands.

- **Milk me.** Some Brits go MIF (milk in first) as opposed to TIF—tea in first. Player's choice.
- **Spooning.** Use your teaspoon to stir tea softly and silently by folding the liquid toward you from the center of the cup. Don't allow the teaspoon to touch the sides or the rim of the cup. When finished, remove the teaspoon and place it on the right side of the tea saucer.
- **Slice versus wedge.** Lemon is offered thinly sliced and placed on a dish near the milk and sugar. Toss it in, as is. Don't squeeze. Warning: Lemon plus milk equals a mess of floating curds. Pick one or the other.
- **Sipping.** Sip tea quietly. Do not gulp and never slurp.
- **How to scarf a scone.** Spread jam, lemon curd and/or Devonshire cream—a thick, "clotted" cream—on your scone. Follow dinner roll protocol with a scone. Break off a bite-sized piece, apply jam, curd, and/or cream, eat and repeat.
- **Finger food.** Little sandwiches cut in quarters and devoid of crusts. Also expect cookies, petit fours, chocolates, and tarts. Oh, do take only one from each selection to make certain everyone has a chance to sample each item.
- **Tiny tongs.** If visible on the three-tiered stand, use the tiny tongs provided, rather than your fingers, to place the items of food on your plate.
- **Disposables.** Don't squeeze tea bags or wave sugar wrappers. Neatly fold and place used items on a side saucer.

Never Let 'Em See You Sweat

As much as the residents of this town enjoy indulging their refined palates, they are even more fanatical with removing any evidence that food consumption has taken place. In Beverly Hills (Los Angeles in general) you can spend six hours a day at a gym and no one will think that's weird. A fully marbleized body is almost as valuable a currency as a title or famous face, one that doesn't rely on talent or connections. Adding gym time to your already stacked schedule is difficult but necessary, hence the popularity of twenty-four-hour establishments. Also, there's always a new work-out trend, which means there's always a *so five minutes ago* workout trend to be discarded. Perhaps you'll want to hire a personal trainer to prevent image disasters, lest you get caught jogging, or doing some other activity reserved for the degenerate masses.

As with any public spectacle, the gym offers the perfect opportunity to pretend to be more important than you really are. To project that image, some will engage in various uncomfortable, forced, and silly behaviors, stomping around as though in a terrible hurry, engaging in loud, dramatic cell phone conversations, and treating gym-goers to bizarrely affectionate greetings. This is particularly hilarious if one treats the gym as a battleground for spouse selection.

- **Appropriate attire.** Are you under the (mistaken) impression that you're at a disco? The beach at St. Tropez? A wet t-shirt contest? Think again.
- **Clean up after yourself.** Return reading materials. Wipe it down. Or up. Any machine you touch. Bacteria is neither imaginary, nor your friend. Utilize strategically placed sanitizing materials before and after. Bring your own towel for anal retentive bonus points.
- **Equipment watch.** Don't highjack the best machine; share. If you've been on the treadmill past your allotted time at rush hour, throwing a towel over the display is a cheesy move. Return free weights to their rightful place.
- **Quiet, please.** Keep dialogue at a low decibel. I'm trying to catch up on my latest issue of *Departures* magazine and would rather not be distracted by your loud chitchat.

- **Locker room nudity.** Are you an exhibitionist, or a voyeur? Please refrain from putting your peccadilloes on display where you have a captive audience.
- **Classes.** Any group activity that offers multiple opportunities to display bad behavior.
- **Don't get territorial.** We are not in kindergarten and you do not own that space.
- **Keep it calm.** Don't bring your despair, anxiety, and rage into your relaxing yoga class (and ruin the Chi for everyone else).
- **Exit strategy.** If you have to leave early, let your instructor know in advance, so he doesn't think he's bored you.

Public Performances

The citizens of Beverly Hills don't have to travel far to get cultured. The recently annointed Wallis Annenberg Center for the Performing Arts allows them to obtain their fix any night of the week in their own backyard. Whether traveling downtown for a night at the LA Opera, to Hollywood to take in a matinée at the Pantages, or over to West LA for a late morning steal into a movie at the Landmark on Pico, here's the rundown on audience etiquette at cultural events.

- **Dress the part.** Select your costume based upon the formality of the event. (Opera night at the Dorothy Chandler Pavilion *in theory* requires a different style of dress than a Beyoncé concert at the Staples Center.) Also, consider any possible destinations before and after the performance (hipster art opening, downtown dive bar?). When in doubt, ask the host.
- **Be punctual.** Allow for enough time to find parking, navigate Will Call, freshen up, schmooze the crowd, and find your seat. This might take *hours*.

- **Take a seat.** When entering a row already full of seated patrons, face those seated (as opposed to treating them to a face full of your backside) and repeat "excuse me" and "thank you" as you move toward your seat. If you need to leave during a performance, repeat the process but *whisper*, along with vague apologies.

Bonus Tip

Movie night out. A night at the movies involves many of the same guidelines as attending any other cultural performance, except the apparently relaxed environment encourages patrons to break more rules. Still, this is a public space, not your living room, so please keep your pants and shoes on, refrain from putting your feet up on the seat in front of you, eat quietly, throw away trash, recycle used 3D glasses, etc.

- **Make it easier for latecomers.** If you are already seated, cut those arriving last minute some slack by creating space and facing your knees in the direction they are moving. This will allow everyone to get seated faster and without fanfare.
- **Silence is golden.** Turn off your mobile devices. No talking, texting, or photos. Once the performance starts, hold your brilliant observations until intermission.
- **Intermission.** Use your time wisely to avoid a panicked return to your seat.
- **Fashionably late.** Stand in the back of the theater and wait for a natural break before making your way to your

seat. Allow the appointed usher to seat you. Avoid grop-
ing other patrons.

- **Tidy up after yourself.** Don't leave your half-empty bag
  of cold popcorn.
- **Exiting.** If you must leave before the performance ends,
  look for a pause in the action and make a stealthy departure.

Bonus Tip

Applaud with aplomb. A word about applause—
there's a gender-based protocol. Choose your gender and applaud appropriately.

- Ladies clap hands by cupping their left hand
  slightly and gently tapping it with the fingers
  of their right hand.
- Gentlemen, clap the two hands together evenly.

Expose Yourself to Art

Contrary to popular thought, the Los Angeles area is an
extremely sophisticated art mecca. Don't miss the Getty,
LACMA, the Hammer, and MOCA. The gallery scene is among
the best in the world. Yes, you may find 99 percent of what
you see pedestrian, weird, disturbing, hideous, or clearly
made by a fifth-grader. Please keep your opinions, while
obviously based on your advanced education and exquisite
taste, at a whisper so you don't ruin the experience for others. Particularly at gallery openings, because the artist, who
sweated and cried and starved and gave up a lucrative career

as a lawyer, breaking his parents' hearts, to make this—his life's work—is standing right next to you. *Sorry.*

- **Eating and drinking.** Must you always be stuffing something in your mouth? If you're starved, hit the museum café for a quiet gourmet bite before you hit the galleries.
- **Photography and video.** Most museums do not permit photographs or videos. Sometimes, special permission may be obtained ahead of time from the curator. Use of flash photography can damage rare paintings. Ask before you snap.
- **Sketching.** Visitors may be allowed to sketch in some museums; however, the museum will dictate what can or cannot be used, such as the type of pencils and sizes of drawing pads.
- **Don't bogart that painting.** Stay at least two feet from artwork so as not to obstruct the view for other visitors.
- **Keep your hands to yourself.** Never touch the art. That painting is five hundred years old! You are able to view it by virtue of all the other people who resisted smearing it with the grime and grape jelly and minute acids living on your fingers.
- **No horseplay around the art.** Of course, those giant Rothkos inspire you to excitement! Refrain from allowing your joy to cause you to explode into any kind of interpretive dance that might send you careening into the art, damaging these incredible works.
- **Mum's the word.** Avoid speaking, crying, laughing, swearing, or screaming too loudly. Library rules: Don't interrupt the *very* deep thoughts others are enjoying.

Home Entertainment

Trust me, you can't compete with the lavishness available here on a weekly, if not nightly, basis. So don't even try. What am I implying? I am implying that it's not uncommon for a party to feature pop stars on stage, water ballet, and oyster bars that extend the entire length of a plane hangar. Dinner parties will likely be catered by famous chefs. Upon entrance to a film premiere party, you could find yourself looking up and seeing actual snow falling on a warm summer night.

Assuming you don't have the budget to hire a million-dollar special effects crew or synchronized swimmers, you will have to rely on the traditional hosting techniques that have produced fun parties since the dawn of mankind. For details, read on.

The Invitation Sets the Tone

Ever wonder why no one RSVPs any more—even though you used an online invitation site with really cute animated graphics? Well, first of all, half your invitations are probably sitting in a spam folder, along with invitations to purchase Viagra and mail-order brides from unspecified international destinations.

Also, we're all a little old-fashioned; an email doesn't quite pack the urgency of response as a written invitation that arrives in the post. A free-for-all invite on Facebook is even more lackluster. Come the day of the event, you might find yourself running out of grass-fed burgers, sweet potato chips, and organic hard cider because everyone who couldn't be bothered to RSVP decided to show up anyway.

If the event is at all formal, or requires an accurate head count for a table setting, opt for the paper treatment. Send out invites two to four weeks in advance for birthday parties and other small gatherings; eight to twelve weeks for weddings and other major celebrations that no one will want to miss because of a scheduling mix-up.

The Social Cost of Not RSVPing

Asking prospective guests to commit in this town is like asking someone to donate blood using the leech method. "I'm not sure," they say, after your fifth phone call. "I'll let you know." In truth, your prospect is weighing your invitation against a pending tennis date with a producer, but secretly hoping a hot lunch with a hotter actress might come through.

The literal translation of RSVP is "respond if you please" and originates from a time when a response was pleasantly suggested, rather than held against us. The current symbolic translation feels a bit like a threat: "Fail to respond, at your peril." Some of us are pleased to reply a few hours before the event (once all the more enticing events have fallen through). According to a recent statistic, more than 80 percent of personal invitations receive no response at all. That's a lot of peril.

- **Keep track of your many invitations.** Once you receive an invitation, you should RSVP within twenty-four to forty-eight hours. In case of conflict, etiquette dictates you RSVP to the first invitation that arrives and decline the subsequent. In any case, use your smart little phone to make sure you don't forget your *yes*.
- **Split your time sensibly.** Double and triple booking is part of the player's handbook, but that's not the book I'm writing. It's nearly impossible to be a *present* participant of any single event when you are dashing from one place to the next! Also, hosts often feel that the first event attended is the less crucial one, because the attendee is clearly saving the best for last. If it will be obvious, give your host a heads-up and make it your business to be the life of the first party.

- **Electronic invites.** Just as binding as a paper invite. The "see who has RSVP'd" feature allows players to decide whether to go, based on who's already coming. The comedy starts because everyone's holding off, because everyone's *holding off.* Yes, the comment feature is fun, plus the automatic reminders are helpful in corralling the space cases.

- **Quid pro quo.** However many individuals you invite to your fundraiser, expect a spate of invitations to theirs in return. You're obligated, especially to those who donated to your cause. Get out your checkbook. Everyone in this town is involved in a charity.

- **Make sure you have a good excuse.** And keep it simple. The more elaborate your lie, the more obvious.

- **Even if you are a VIP, don't behave like an ASS.** Unless you are the President of the United States, your RSVP is required, like everyone else. We all have insanely busy social calendars. I know you are so very popular. Congratulations.

- **Some of your closest friends might be the worst offenders.** The first to take your relationship for granted. Yes, this is aimed at you, in case *you're* the worst offender.

Dinner Party Circuit

As I may have mentioned, this is the capital of nepotism and word-of-mouth. The constant fear of climbers, stalkers, gossips, spies, bloggers, and journalists means that every single connection is made on a friend-of-friend basis. Trust is everything. If you don't arrive with a built-in social set, you'd better be a social super-electro-magnet: stunningly gorgeous, wildly witty, with military-style training in etiquette.

The hotbed of social connections is the dinner party circuit. Dinner parties are better than cocktail parties because they avail you serious face time, drawn out over hours. You may distinguish yourself in a ten-minute conversation at a party, but you were just a pleasant distraction. Dinner party guest lists are designed with the express intent of sparking a connection. It's how a serial yenta executes successful match-ups, how a film producer packages a team. As a host or guest, you'll want to give as good as you get.

Outtake

Host a Marvelous Dinner Party

A great host might explode with stress during prep, but the minute the doorbell rings, it will be all smiles, warm welcomes, and flawless, 100 percent zen calm, even if everything goes totally awry. Nothing should disarm the host—an incinerated roast, a tray of flying wine glasses shattering across a room, not even a fist fight if exes accidentally collide. Mishaps handled with humor add to the flavor and color of an event.

We host to put our best qualities on display. While these qualities may include our good taste, grasp of culinary skill, and meticulously culled decor, it's the subtle ways in which we make a guest feel comfortable that make an event memorable. If you allow your guests to feel your tension, you might as well throw a cold, dead carp on a platter and serve it. Partygoers would prefer swilling convenience store twelve-packs and crunching stale potato chips in an abandoned parking lot than dining on champagne and crab cakes at an estate, if those crab cakes are served with a sour face and a heaping plate of hysteria. Serve these instead:

- **Generosity.** Hosts spare no detail to accommodate their guests' comfort and enjoyment. There will be adequate supplies of everything on hand.

- **Expert choreography.** Hosts do as much prep pre-party as possible to maximize social contact with guests during the event.
- **Beauty.** Good advance work means hosts will have moments to relax and use the time to attend to looking fantastic.
- **A warm welcome.** Hosts offer guests a drink immediately upon arrival and offer to take coats and purses. If it's cold, the fireplace will be roaring. The lights won't be glaring. The music won't be blaring.
- **Social opportunity.** Use place cards at a large sit-down dinner so guests aren't shuffling in confusion at table time. Keep couples separate, spark new connections and checkerboard genders. Also, group together guests by interests. Put introverts near the center and the gregarious (loud, excitable) guests toward the end of the table. The host is always nearest to the door or kitchen.
- **Grace.** Unless it's a potluck, hosts decline any offers of financial contribution. We never allow our guests to worry about the cost of an evening because that would interfere with their enjoyment.

Bonus Tip

Sock hop. The practice of leaving your shoes at the door is adopted from a traditional Japanese custom. While a host may prefer bare feet on his or her recently refinished wood floors, guests in America like to leave their shoes on, especially women who like to show off their new designer shoes. That woman would be me.

- **Selflessness.** Hosts know their guests' likes and dislikes in advance. A bit of research helps planning the menu, bearing in mind any food allergies, dietary restrictions, and other insanities.
- **Indulgence.** Hosts go beyond expectations to see to guests' needs and wants and whims. If a guest drinks only green tea, it will be waiting in a fresh, steaming pot.

Outtake

Be a Fabulous Dinner Guest

Congratulations! Your hard work at self-branding has paid off, and you've been invited to dip your toe in the dinner party pool. Let's put all your dining etiquette training and conversational skills to work and see if you don't walk out of that party with a three-picture deal.

- **Go with the flow.** Assuming your hosts are not planning something highly inappropriate or completely insane, why not go along and make them happy? If it's a theme dinner, then play along and dress accordingly. If it's a hike with a picnic lunch, then lace up your boots and pace yourself going up the hill.
- **Bring a token of your gratitude.** Bring a bottle, buy a pie, or pillage the neighbor's rose bush. Never show up empty handed. A little personalized gift can go a long way toward getting invited next time.
- **Jump in, superguest.** Unless the affair is fully catered, or you'll be in the way, offer to roll up your sleeves and help in the kitchen. Be the first to stand up and help clear plates (once everyone's obviously done eating!). Serve from the left, clear from the right.

- **Clink!** If a toast is given, pay attention and respond accordingly with a rousing "cheers," "here, here," or whatever else floats your boat.
- **Say thanks with meaning.** After the dessert plates have been cleared and the stimulating conversation has slowed to small pleasantries and vicious, drunken gossip, it is time to say goodbye. After all, the key to a perfect evening is knowing when to make your exit. Time it so that you have not overstayed your welcome, but have made your host feel as though the evening was a success.

Mutually Exclusive: A Day at the Country Club

Yes, we have a lot in common with the Midwest—for one, we have snotty country clubs. Well, Beverly Hills has one with a golf course; the other's just a tennis club. But it's just like *Caddyshack*. Mile-long brunch buffets, vicious games of Mahjong, ruthless smack downs for tennis and golf trophies, petty scrimmages between the old guard and the young families. Favors and vendettas influence membership applications for decades; be careful whom you cut off in traffic. There are only two days where unruly children are to be seen *and* heard—Easter Sunday and the day they hire the down-and-out Santa Claus.

- **Idiosyncratic dress code warnings.** Many clubs have a policy banning jeans, shorts, and cargo pants (I, too, have a policy banning cargo pants). Shirts should be tucked in and secured with a belt, despite your husband's protruding muffin-top. No hats allowed in dining areas. No cowboy hats, no hard hats, no sailor's caps.
- **Golf.** You'll be expected to wear a shirt with a collar, change your shoes in the locker room, check in at the pro shop, and bring your own set of clubs. Also, please

don't wear orange plaid pants and drive the golf cart like a drunken maniac.

- **Tipping.** Yes. Generously. To anyone who lifts a finger to help you. Be the 1 percent of the 1 percent who doesn't act like an a-hole.
- **Tennis.** Please note that John McEnroe's famous on-court explosions of expletives and racquet bashing are fun to practice in the privacy of your own home, not the club court.
- **Poolside.** The pool isn't a mosh pit where diving into the crowd is applauded.
- **Locker room.** Don't leave that wet towel on the ground. And if you've left bunches of hair in the bathroom, for Chrissake, remove it to the trash. This isn't a hotel.
- **Cell phones.** This is my club, this is my sanctuary; I don't want to hear your phone conversation, thank you.
- **Staff.** We *love* the staff, from the groundskeepers to the general manager, so we always smile and say hello.
- **Complaints.** No trashing other members over iced tea; take your petty, catty disputes directly to management.
- **Thank you.** Even if you're a guest of the most obnoxiously moneyed person you know, you must still offer to pay for whatever charges you incur. Also, if you had a spectacular day at the club, send your appreciation to the host via a handwritten note. You just must.

High Social Anxiety

For some reason, a social gathering can inspire quite a bit of anxiety, even among seasoned adults. Some of us turn into shy, embarrassed, and self-conscious three-year-olds who would rather skip a great party than face that inner monologue of insecurities:

Why did I wear this? I look like a giant peppermint marshmallow.
I'm so boring, kill me now.
I can't leave the house. The bruise from my Botox treatment is still showing.
Everyone here has an Oscar and I just sold my car to pay the sound guy on my first film.

Pfft. I'm always in the mood to celebrate. Bridal shower, fundraiser, Tupperware party. I'm there, with bells on. Doesn't mean I'm a picture of calm, cool, and collected when I walk through that front door. In fact, I can leave the house feeling like a rock star, only to arrive and suddenly feel like I'm nothing but a washed-out roadie.

Thankfully, my classes on social anxiety have rubbed off on me and I always carry an imaginary tool belt to deal with any last-minute image crises:

- **Select the proper costume.** When you walk into a room crowded with strangers, your outfit will make your first impression for you. Start with the host's intention and find the intersection between your signature style and what's expected of you. And there will be *actual* costume epics, as well; oh, don't spoil it by refusing to follow the theme. Put on that gorilla suit and go to town.
- **Never arrive empty-handed.** Bring a festive bottle or an imaginative gift that sparks conversation. Something splashy, but not absurdly expensive, will give your front door entrance a little extra *pizazz*.
- **Flip the switch to "on."** Everyone has troubles; please conveniently forget to bring yours. The purpose of parties is to drown our sorrows. So start drowning other people's sorrows with buckets of fun.

- **Don't enter the party starving.** A blood sugar crash will crush your wit.
- **Carbonated beverages.** Avoid, because this isn't the fraternity and a burp doesn't make good punctuation to a sentence.
- **Scan the room for anyone you know.** If you come up short, introduce yourself to anyone who makes eye contact. Shove out that right hand for the perfect handshake.
- **Say thanks and depart discreetly.** Ever noticed how one person's loud exit will trigger a mass exodus? At large parties, it's better to slip out without a word. This is called the "French leave," and it is perfectly acceptable and avoids the domino effect of a party cut short before its time. For smaller parties, it's critical to thank your host for the fabulous time you had. If you want to get another invite, a thank-you call or note is a superb finish to your performance.

The Dreaded One-on-One

Okay, you're in a room filled with intimidating strangers, all exchanging inside jokes and eyeing you as though you might be a party crasher, or worse, a *blogger*. Listen, this town lives on soy lattés and sound bites. We're starved for rich, high-calorie conversation, and if you have that to offer, you'll never be short on invitations.

Good conversation is ideally equal parts listening and talking, interesting and interested, and never a battle for oxygen (but here in the city of all-consuming egos, that's not always possible). A good strategy for infiltration is to gently ask simple questions that deflect attention away from you and back toward those who crave it most—everyone else in the room. In this town, actually in every town, people are by and large in love with themselves. The sound of their own voice makes them swoon, and they are dying to trumpet their accomplishments. Let them! Make way for the monologue. All you have to do is nod and smile. Easy. The talker will walk away from you, thinking, "Oh my God, she's *awesome*."

In this vein, your most reliable breaking and entering scheme would be to locate the nearest self-aggrandizing loudmouth in the room (that won't take long) and allow them to share freely, treating you and everyone else in earshot to a recitation of their recent victories. You don't need to tell people your life story at parties; that's what your $500/hour shrink is for.

Punctuate the conversation, don't dominate it.

A knack for observation goes a long way. Your conversation partner is sporting a fabulous tan—did he just return from vacation? *Golf weekend in Palm Springs*, he replies. (Although more likely a strip-mall tanning salon in Calabasas, but we play along, nonetheless.) You've got two openings then: chat up the oasis two hours east on the 10 Freeway or riff on the sport of golf. And you know nothing of golf. "Oh, I love Palm Springs," you say. "Have you ever been to that terrific Mexican restaurant in Rancho Mirage?"

Take it from there. Party conversations are a perfect way to expand your world. Make a habit of discovering what your conversation partners are passionate about. Find things in common, obtain useful rumors, and collect obscure factoids. Everyone, and I mean *everyone*, possesses some interesting experience or expertise about something.

Outtake

Ice-breakers
Starting off with a neutral compliment is a useful opener: "What's the story behind that amazing (article of clothing, jewelry, or

hat)?" *What's the story* gives the other person permission to speak freely, at length. Oh, and they will.

- **Get in sync.** Match your partner's rhythm and pace of speech—speed up, slow down accordingly. Also, mirror their movements and mannerisms ever so slightly, as if you're dancing—you'll find it's a subtle way of building rapport.
- **Express interest.** Lean forward to express interest, nod in agreement.
- **Listen actively.** Clear your head so your inner dialogue doesn't interrupt your conversation partner.
- **Think before speaking.** Engage and be engaged! Rehearse what you're about to say (without being obvious). The more you do that, the better you'll be off the cuff and less likely to put your foot in your mouth.
- **Be precise.** Don't ramble. People are busy. Make your point and get out.
- **Spice up your vocabulary.** Try for a better response than repeating "That's cool" again and again. Ask a follow-up question instead.
- **Don't enjoy bringing the bad news.** If you have something nasty to say, by all means, spare everyone and sugarcoat it.
- **Accept compliments with grace.** Don't deflect or contradict a compliment. But do use the moment to boost the hard work of others. "Thank you, it took years to get that movie made and a lot of good people helped out."
- **Be prepared for topical conversation.** Please know something about the world. Read a book, read the news online. Weather is actually fascinating. Other safe topics: holidays, travel, sports, change of season.
- **Talk about TV and movies.** This is the one place in the world where you're not a total loser for knowing every

television show that's on the air and every movie ever made.

- **But beware of trashing these same shows and movies.** Someone in the room probably worked on whatever it is you're describing in such unflattering terms.
- **End a conversation on a high note.** Leave before the pauses outnumber the words. Finish your drink, pretend it's time to go get another one. Or step back and offer to exchange contact information. "So nice to talk to you! Sorry, I need to say hello to Max over there before he leaves." Do you even know Max? No. But you're hoping he'll read your script.

Bonus Tip

Verbal faux pas. We all do it, from time to time: say the wrong thing completely unintentionally. Just don't make it your signature habit. It might be a condescending little act of contradiction, like correcting someone's grammar or a bit of unsolicited fact-checking in the moment. You might strike a nerve with a question that goes over the line. You think you're paying a compliment when you tell someone he or she's lost weight. Here's what the recipient heard: "Oh, you used to be a lot fatter." Try "You look fantastic," and leave it at that. Also, never ask the following question: "So, what do you do?" Everyone knows what you're really asking: "How much money do you make?"

Outtake

Conversation Killers

In my short life, we've devolved from acronyms to emoticons, using a lexicon of abbreviations as an unacceptable substitute for complex, interesting ideas. We've become, like, a total nation of *teenagers*—slang-centric, disrespectful, often impossible to understand, and open to extreme interpretation. *Ummm* . . . is not a word, it's a mantra.

- **Don't launch your conversation with something too controversial.** You risk a quickly degenerating debate over politics and/or religion.
- **Hold off asking probing questions.** You are guaranteed to touch a nerve.
- **This isn't a talk show.** Don't get too boisterous about your opinions regarding art, fashion, or film. In polite conversation, this behavior gives everyone the (wrong, I hope) impression that you're absolutely annoying.
- **Suppress the need to overshare.** It comes off as creepy. And I'm not your shrink.
- **Don't make assumptions.** People hate it when they're reduced, judged, or packaged.
- **Be aware of potentially annoying habits and mannerisms.** You have one shot to charm someone with your amusing repartee—don't muck it up by smacking your gum, tapping your toes, or cracking your knuckles.
- **Don't invade space.** No one likes it when someone gets in your face. Keep 18 inches (about an arm's length) away from your conversation partners (unless you're in a packed party or an elevator). If someone does it to you, step back with one foot and angle out, as many times as you have to.
- **Avoid cheap fillers.** Strike the word "like" from your vocabulary. You are, *like*, not striving to be *like* anyone or

anything else. Don't begin every sentence with, "The bottom line is" and don't finish every statement with, "You know what I mean?"

- **Skip foreign slang.** Never, ever try to speak to someone outside your culture in what you perceive to be their vernacular, whether it be teenagers, gang members, or the French.
- **Forget all foul language in public.** Unless the script calls for it.
- **Avoid excess flattery.** It will get you nowhere in this town, since everyone already knows how great they are.
- **Don't interrupt.** I know your thoughts are so important and timely, but if you interrupt people, that is all they'll remember. Not the brilliant thing you said. Just that you were rude.
- **Easy on the jokes.** Yikes. Unless you're a professional. In which case, you don't want to give it away for free, do you?
- **Never be mean.** If you're going to say something critical, make it the funniest, classiest putdown ever—the kind that will make your object of derision *love* you (not hate you!).

Bonus Tip

Body language is universal. Most people are highly unaware of the message they are communicating with their bodies. They have no clue that their facial expressions, hand gestures, and other body movements are making an impression on others, and it's not always a good one. Make yourself the most approachable with an inviting smile and relaxed body posture. Shun the sour-puss face and crossed-arms syndrome at all costs.

6

Stress-Free Holidays

(There's no such thing.)

Every year, it starts right after Halloween. The candy corn goes half-price, the Christmas carols start pumping from invisible store speakers, and we start bracing for the holiday marathon. Thanksgiving is a game of musical chairs as you scout your last-minute invitations or hit LAX for the worst travel weekend of the year. Then it's frantic Black Friday shopping and a slew of party obligations. The day-after-Christmas sales serve only to launch another retail madhouse slap fight. That leaves a few days of post-party depression, cataloging the year's regrets, before the final push for New Year's Eve, which will be the usual letdown.

It's the time of year when this town's devotion to materialism (and disparity) shows itself in full contrast. The store windows on Rodeo Drive will feature absurdly lavish seasonal displays, and rumors will spread of enormous gifts largesse. Some actress will go on a $75,000 shopping spree at Neiman's, and by the time you hear about it from your manicurist, the damage will have become $250,000. The entertainment companies will send out rich, personalized tokens of the season to their clients and associates, while the gift baskets from desperate vendors will stack up in the mailroom. Gift distribution will establish the year's hierarchy forecast. *I haven't received my gift from CAA yet!* (Subtitle: *Oh my God, when did I become B-list?*)

Corporate business comes to a complete stop. Smart executives take off the month of December, flying away to Morocco or Gstaad or the Seychelles and leaving the help to man the phones, solve the crises, make sure the A-list is covered, and then make fools of themselves at the company parties.

Let the games begin!

Shopping without Dropping

Thanks to online retail, it's the delivery companies who now bear most of the gravity of the season. However, you still have to venture out to obtain wrapping paper, cards, last-minute gifts, and an endless supply of cocktail nuts. Even the most assiduous online shopper can't do it all from an iPad.

- **Power up.** Keep a KIND Bar stashed, because a rock-bottom blood sugar crash will do nothing to help you deal with long lines, no parking, screaming infants, and avaricious shoppers stressed to the point of violence.
- **Avoid confrontation.** It's the holidays, for gosh-sakes. Spread cheer, not fear.
- **Get zen about lines.** The grocery store, the dry-cleaner, and the big box stores will all be cage-fight arenas for

pushing, crowding, and hurry-up-and-waiting. Please don't cut, force, shove, or sigh loudly. If your shopping cart is packed and someone behind you has one or two items, let them go ahead. Again, it's the *holidays*. And once you're at the cashier, avoid prolonged chitter-chatter. Just because you waited for thirty minutes doesn't entitle you to abuse your turn.

- **Be tolerant with transgressors.** It's the season of giving, right? We're all stressed beyond belief. That lady who bumped into you with her cart because she was rubbernecking the microwavable heat wraps? Her alcoholic, chain-smoking in-laws are arriving from Duluth in two hours and this is her last chance to fill her badly needed prescription for Xanax. On that note . . .

The Family Trap

They're all you've got, honey. Family. If you can get together without a trip to the nearest hospital, consider yourself lucky. It may be a blessing in an elaborate disguise, as you circumvent your husband's openly seething hatred for your mother, or grandpa's flagrant racist remarks that are more appropriate to another century.

- **Make it a formal affair.** Insist everyone dress for events. The strategy: Your family members will feel less comfortable, and therefore less likely to fall into their usual (confrontational, boundary-pushing, bratty) roles.
- **Inject humor wherever possible.** However possible. Pop in a funny holiday movie (there are a slew of good options), offer up a game of charades, crack a joke. Do something to break the tension. People who are sharing a laugh are less likely to get into knockdown, drag-out family fights.

- **Take your finger off the button.** Family members are acutely aware of the most effective triggers that will detonate emotional explosions, and there's always at least one member of the tribe who loves that kind of floorshow. If it's you, create an obsessive-compulsive ritual to distract yourself from starting something. Please.
- **Shower with compliments.** Even if you have to lie, just for a few hours, idle flattery and a blithe spirit is better than the biting, vulgar, vicious remarks you tend to make every other night of the year.
- **Gratitude attitude.** Consider that this might be Uncle Manny's last Hanukkah, so please refrain from ridiculing your sister about her appalling dating choices at the dinner table. Save that for a nightcap in the pool house.

Everyone's on good behavior until one of the older statesmen in the family gets sick, especially one with an estate to inherit. That's when all hell breaks loose and it's a feeding frenzy.

> *I once coached the owner of a nursing care facility for billionaires. Frankly, the problem wasn't the elderly patients, but the offspring— the billionaires waiting to happen—who were actually upset with the owner for prolonging their parents' lives with expert care. Diplomacy was the assignment here.*

The Holiday Gift Extravaganza

With friends and family, there's one rule and one rule only: It's the message that matters. Sometimes that message might be: *I don't really know you and given a budget of $500, this is what the store clerk pointed at while he was helping three other customers, voilá!* That's your business. If you're seeking a more personalized way of expressing your appreciation for friends or family or business associates, become the sort of thoughtful individual who routinely jumps on the perfect gift when you see it on your travails throughout the year. Accompany it with a great one-liner in a card, and wow! A word of warning: Professionals keep careful gift records of who and what and when to avoid duplications and re-gifting debacles.

Let's get to holiday tipping for the staff: the nanny who's basically raising your children; the doorman whose discretion you count on more often than you'd like; the caregiver who sponge-bathes your ailing father so you can blow in, say a few friendly words, and go on with your day.

- **Cash.** Is cash cold and hard? No, not if the recipient is busting backside for six bucks an hour and counts on that second or third job to pay the utilities. Add a small gift to show you *care*.
- **Cards.** If cash looks tacky, there are hundreds of gift cards to suit your dog walker, your kid's long-suffering teacher, the girl who grins and bears it as she gives you a *thorough* waxing.
- **Creativity.** Craft night is so hipster. Flowers made of felt or homemade gluten-free confections wrapped with a ribbon are a great add-on/substitution when cash flow is low or for the person who has virtually everything and is difficult to please. (Who can say no to something made from the heart? Someone *heartless*.)
- **Gifts.** Unique or something you are confident the recipient will enjoy. Never on sale, that is just gauche (not to be confused with Gaché!). Many stores will not accept a returned item that is purchased on sale. Save yourself being labeled cheap and get something for full price, for goodness' sake.

Holiday Tipping Tips:

Service Provider	Suggested Cash Tip
Building Staff	$20–$100 (depends on how often you call upon their services)
Dog Walker, Pet Sitter	One Week's Service
Doorman	$25–$200 (varies in metropolitan areas)
Full-Time Babysitter or Nanny	One to Two Week's Pay (plus small gift from children)
Gardener	Cost of One Visit
Hair Stylist/Barber	Equivalent of One Service
Housekeeper	One Week's Pay
Manicurist	Cost of One Session
Massage Therapist	Cost of One Session
Newspaper Carrier	Daily Deliveries $25 / Weekends Only $10–$15
Personal Trainer	Cost of One Session or One Week's Visit
Postman	A small gift or gift card of less than $20
Private Home Nurse or Caregiver	One Week's Pay (check with agency to make sure it is accepted)
Teachers	Gift Card ($25–$50 is an acceptable range)
Trash Collectors	$10–$20 each (check with your local city)

- **New Year's gifts.** Avoid the multicultural "what holiday do you celebrate" confusion by sending a Happy New

Year package. Take note, it will be understood that any gift that goes along will have been re-gifted. Which leads me to . . .

Rules of Re-gifting

Be careful! If you're found out, you might as well move to Monrovia. Acceptable circumstances for re-gifting include financial woes, last-minute hostess gifting, charity items, and secret holiday gift exchanges.

- **Inspect each item carefully.** Conduct the equivalent of a radiation scrub down by removing all signs of previous ownership. Make sure there is no hidden writing with a personalized message, monogram, or name. There should be no evidence of prior wrapping or torn packaging from the original recipient.
- **Re-gift new items.** Worst-case scenario: an item you found in the garage from a store that no longer exists. Unless clearly *vintage*, have the smarts to re-gift something purchased within the same calendar year.
- **Some items should never be re-gifted.** Anything clearly showing use or anything so personalized that it can be tracked back to its origin. Any gift received from your mother-in-law. You wouldn't want your housekeeper accidentally wearing the Old Navy sweater you re-gifted to her the next time the matron of the family pays you a visit.
- **Make the re-gift look spectacular.** If you re-gift an item, at least take the time to rewrap it as nicely as possible.
- **Accept re-gifts graciously.** If you get one, and you like the gift, take it. Love it. Wear it proudly. If it's not your cup of tea, smile and say *thank you* anyway.

Beware the Office Party

I generally advise partygoers in this town to down a few espressos and some protein bars (followed by copious breath mintage) before arriving to any work gathering rather than a series of alcoholic beverages that will leave you slow-witted, tongue-tied, and a little over-affectionate. Save your sorrow-drowning for the privacy of your own home. This is your career on the line. This office party is your *in* to freely socialize with higher-ups. In other words, it's an opportunity to network, to advance and shine. Repress the need to let off some steam at any office get-together, especially at the holidays where the punch is flowing and the punches might start flying. Think this is your big blowout after a hard year slogging in the trenches? Yes, you blew something. It was your career.

- **Dress.** This is not the time to *let your freak flag fly* as they used to say, especially if you give your officemates the impression that you regularly pick up a few extra bucks working Hollywood Boulevard on Saturday nights. And this goes for women, as well as men!
- **Booze ration.** I don't care if there's an open bar stocked with top-shelf bottles, and you can only afford bottom shelf—make that highball last all night. Keep yourself hydrated by filling it with ice and water. You will not be sorry when you see James, that nice young man from accounting, dancing on the conference table and drunkenly mimicking the CEO, who is staring at him now, aghast, because James failed to read these words.
- **Overstuffing.** This is not a stock-up for a hurricane. It can get weird watching people gorge themselves. Especially when they try to talk at the same time.

- **Self-control.** Avoid hitting on your office crush on the dance floor with everyone watching because you've downed a bucket of liquid courage (liquid *insanity!*).
- **Badmouthing.** Don't let loose with your opinions, the ones you've kept bottled up, all year, under lock and key. P.S., if you badmouth anyone, others will assume logically you badmouth them.
- **Secret Santa shame.** Don't re-gift a gag item from the Hustler store. Enough said.
- **Recognition.** A nice note sent to the person responsible for organizing that *lavish, splendiferous, super fun* office party would never be wrong in any town, on any planet.

7

Happy Houseguesting

Oh good for you, you've fallen in with the summerhouse set. Yes, the crowd that maintains second and third residences the way we might collect kids' bicycles in the side yard. Suddenly, you find yourself invited to a sojourn in Palm Springs or the Hamptons, in Santa Barbara or Sun Valley, or any one of Hawaii's many islands.

Or, perhaps you are just moving to a new town and crashing with a buddy while you look for a job and your own place. We both know that will take longer than a weekend. Keep reading. The rules apply to you, as well.

Here in Beverly Hills, most houses have something in the backyard designated as a guesthouse. It may be a glorified pool cabana or its own little manse, (which your host will nevertheless call "the cottage"). Our town's down and outs might rent out their cottages for a sweet monthly paycheck (now that the alimony's dried up). Renters think they're getting their own little slice of heaven, but end up spending an agonizing amount of time listening to a former starlet, now alcoholic senior with skin the consistency of turkey jerky, rasping about ex-husbands between drags on an endless cigarette. You'll slowly become aware that your rent checks are going straight to a disgraced plastic surgeon.

This, by the way, is your most likely introduction to Beverly Hills. But I digress.

Let's say you've been graced with an invitation to spend a long weekend in someone else's home or guesthouse. Do not take this lightly. You have been judged as civilized and this judgment obligates you to bring your congenial and mannered self, not the messy, lazy, slipper-wearing late sleeper that you actually are.

In other words, you are marching off to war, a war of attrition.

Your hosts will wear you down with their early breakfast calls, excursions to scenic attractions, inane competitions (a family tradition!), and possible exposure to edibles you wouldn't touch even as a well-paid reality show star. In short, you will be held captive in a foreign culture, with no escape until 11:59 a.m. Sunday morning.

Good Guest Check List:

- **Invest in decent luggage.** I know you typically throw your clothes into a plastic garbage bag, but if you've been invited to vacation at a civilized home, you will be making the investment in one or two luggage bags, preferably matching and with wheels. Pack for various occasions. A weekend bag is perfect for a short stay. No matter what, never arrive with a king-size duffel bag. You're not moving in.
- **A small gift goes a long way.** Choose a nice hostess gift and present it upon arrival. A bottle of this, a jar of that,

a small something for the kids. An expensive little candle will do (they're all expensive these days), but refrain from trying to redecorate your host's house.

* **You have not checked into a hotel.** Even if you are staying at a glorious estate, employing scores of staff all too happy to see to your needs, they are not at your disposal, beck, or call. Be as polite to them as you are to your hosts. Offer to help, even if you find yourself in a kitchen full of help.

* **A houseguest always dresses.** It may be the weekend, but think work attire, not gym-wear. You may relax in your mind, but not in your style and attitude. Coiff, comb, and keep it clipped for the weekend.

* **Contribute generously.** An offer to pitch in with grocery purchases is a perfect gesture. A superb guest might also show his or her appreciation by picking up a dinner tab.

* **Adapt to your host's daily routine.** If breakfast is served at eight, be at the table at eight with bells on. Although you might think yoga is the domain of absurd Santa Monica housewives, if your host invites you to downward dog, then *namaste* like a good boy.

* **The host is always right.** Even if your host's political views (or let's say your host's elderly parent's views) incite you to a murderous rage, you will be just as charming as if you two worked side-by-side on a candidate's campaign. You can have the conversation you wanted to have, in the car, all the way home, by yourself, screaming if you must.

* **Yes, it can be exhausting.** Always being helpful and cheerful and tidy and witty. Which brings me to the next point . . .

* **A good houseguest knows when to depart.** If your hosts beg, on bended knee, swearing on stacks of vintage

Billy Wilder scripts for you to stay an extra day or two, it's up to you. I would only remind you of the reliable old adage regarding leaving them wanting more.

The Never-Coming-Back List of Things to Do:

- **Monopolize the bathroom.** Don't let others know you're *that* kind of person.
- **Allow your mobile device to emit one single sound.** Make calls in the privacy of your room or in some private corner of the estate during a break in the socializing. Keep your voice down. Refrain from trashing anyone. The Hills have ears.
- **Go rogue.** Your hosts have gone to bed, now it's time to slip out the window and hit some bars with some fun people you chatted up in the local grocery store. Actually, if you get a really great invitation, you are obligated to invite your hosts.
- **Forget to write a lovely thank-you note.** Thank your host for that rousing game of table tennis and the valuable advice regarding your lack of a career.

8

The Cordial Bride

Ever witness a bride explode into a control rampage, battling in-laws, bakers, and flower arrangers, the air thick with dread and tension? Okay, that was on television. But it happens. You may feel like a princess on your big day, and most likely you look like one, but this is no coronation.

The truth about weddings: endless meetings, financial considerations, countless decisions, exhausting parties. Wasn't this meant to be a celebration of love and trust and family? Yes, and it's a serious achievement if you can keep those ideals at the forefront as you plod through this process with your loved ones. Nothing prepares you for the ups and downs of marriage like the lead up to a modern wedding. If you still want to get married by your wedding day, by God, it's *real*.

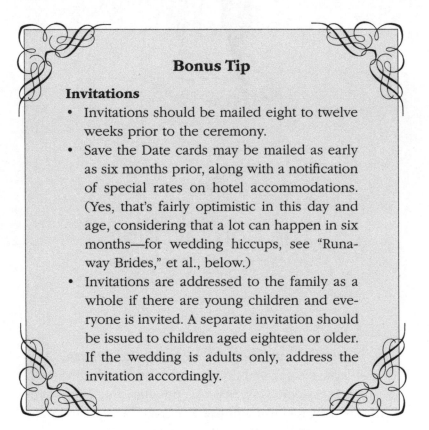

Bonus Tip

Invitations

- Invitations should be mailed eight to twelve weeks prior to the ceremony.
- Save the Date cards may be mailed as early as six months prior, along with a notification of special rates on hotel accommodations. (Yes, that's fairly optimistic in this day and age, considering that a lot can happen in six months—for wedding hiccups, see "Runaway Brides," et al., below.)
- Invitations are addressed to the family as a whole if there are young children and everyone is invited. A separate invitation should be issued to children aged eighteen or older. If the wedding is adults only, address the invitation accordingly.

Family, Stress, Money: Who Pays for What?

While family involvement may seem to amplify your stresses (approximately 10× for each in-law) who else is going to pick up the tab? You'll quickly come to the (correct) conclusion that this rich pageant is all about them, not you. And that's a healthy attitude—facing reality always is. Here's a rundown on traditions regarding who gets the bill. It's worth noting that times have changed (they have a way of doing that) and it's perfectly acceptable for anyone to pay (anyone with approximately $100,000 to blow on a costume party). A combination of family members may graciously step up and pony up. In any case:

- **The engagement announcement.** Typically the groom's mother should extend the first invitation.
- **The engagement party.** The bride's parents.
- **A wedding shower.** Traditionally, the maid of honor, but it's not unheard of for the mother and/or sister of the bride to host these days; for an out-of-town bride, the groom's mother/sister.
- **Actual ceremony and reception.** The bride's family traditionally pays for everything.
- **The groom's responsibility.** The marriage license, the bride's ring, a gift to the bride, the officiant's fee, and gifts for his attendants.
- **The groom's family.** They pay for the rehearsal dinner, the honeymoon, and the hotel accommodations for his side of the family.

Outtake

How Not to Ruin Someone's Nuptials

- **The RSVP card.** Return it, with your answer, within a forty-eight-hour time period, if at all possible.
- **If you receive a wedding invitation, you send a gift.** Whether you attend or not. The registry service will take care of details. Please buy from that list. If you want to include something personal—a strange portrait of the couple you painted, for example—make it an addition, not a substitution.
- **Gift timing.** The best time to send a gift is when the wedding invitation arrives. However, gifts may arrive afterward, as well, within three months of the wedding.

There is a myth that you have up to one year to send a wedding gift; sorry, that's no longer true thanks to the ease of online wedding registries.

- **Gift amount.** As I suggested in the *Los Angeles Times* during a frenzy over the Princess Kate and Prince William nuptials, "For this kind of a wedding—for any kind of royal wedding—it is considered a great honor. In order to show or convey respect and that gracious feeling for being invited, the ante is a bit more." In other words, don't haggle over a wedding gift; be grateful you were included.
- **Award them with your full attention and turn off your phones during the ceremony!**

The Overexposed Wedding

On a good day, social media keeps us once, twice, and often thrice removed from our lives. Don't let it detract from your big day. Use, but don't abuse, these valuable tools. Couples announce their engagement on Facebook and Twitter and organize details on the web. Sometimes disseminating information in this manner can lead to unintentional blunders. Please tread carefully. Emotions are already running at the boiling point.

- **Slow-drip the news.** Before blasting the fabulous bulletin about your recent engagement to everyone you know on Facebook, be sure to reach out to your nearest and dearest group first, either by phone or personally. Family members and your closest friends will appreciate getting the news before the rest of the world. Beware, however, that once you post your engagement on a social networking site, all that view it may expect an invitation to the wedding. Oops. Speaking of the wedding, it is perfectly fine to post your wedding date online because everyone will want to know, but you should refrain from posting specific details about the ceremony or reception, as that information should be reserved for the mailed invitations.

- **Create a one-stop online wedding shop.** Your own wedding website allows you to post all the details about your wedding in one place. Once you are set up, every feature of your wedding may be organized here, from the suggested attire and wedding venue directions to the bridal party information and the couple's registry. Importantly, particularly if you expect paparazzi (or bitter exes to disrupt the proceedings, renting a marching band to parade down the street, for example), some websites even offer to password-protect your site to ensure no unsolicited traffic. Include the link on your Save the Date cards, not on your Facebook.
- **Potential dangers of digital drift.** The stress of planning and the inevitable conflicts that result should never be grist for Facebook. Ever. Little announcements and comments for your guest list should stay private. Post the (tasteful) photos of the wedding events on Facebook; you didn't invite the world, but the world might want to live vicariously and wish you congratulations. And please don't tweet every moment of your wedding. Focus on experiencing this event, not recording it. That is why you hire a wedding photographer or designate a guest tweeter if that's the generation you come from.

Bachelorette Party Debacles

I will refrain from commenting on *bachelor* parties, because whatever I say will not compete with your repeated viewings of *The Hangover*. Yes, it's an evening designed for debauchery, but please, let the really down and dirty activities remain a fiction for the big screen (and not on the small one, as in photos taken by someone's smartphone and immediately posted online). Imagine embarrassing party videos uploaded to Facebook viewed decades from now by future employers and grandchildren. Keep copyright control. Let's go straight to:

The Do Not List:

- **Leave the guest list in the hands of others.** Make sure that all attendees of the bachelorette party are actually invited to the wedding. It should be comprised of good friends, the bridal party, and other close female relatives. Don't forget to include the mother of the bride and the mother-in-law-to-be. Even if you plan on pulling an all-nighter with your girlfriends, it is appropriate (and expected) to invite them to join you for a pleasant dinner beforehand. An ideal number for a bachelorette party is about ten to twelve, in total, a manageable number for any transportation, dinner, or activities you may be planning.

- **Pick the wrong date.** A bachelorette party is typically planned by the bride-to-be's close circle of friends or relatives. If you are involved in planning, check in with the happy couple to make sure that the bride and groom are even comfortable with the idea. As you are considering dates for the party, ask the bride-to-be if she would prefer having her bachelorette party on the same day as the bachelor party—a good idea, especially if schedules are tight. Setting a date one month in advance is a practical goal. Do *not* schedule the bachelorette party the weekend of the wedding. The last thing a bride needs is a splitting headache, swollen eyes, and possible injuries from a crazy night out with her gal pals.

- **Break the bank.** The bachelorette party is typically paid for by attendees; therefore, planning should be arranged for the tightest pocketbook, not the loosest. Don't arrange an expensive evening, complete with a chauffeured limo and French champagne, unless someone in the party just got a massive commencement check for film work and is willing to treat. Get creative. You can still raise the roof without having to mortgage your home.

- **Choose embarrassing activities.** Don't assume all attendees are up for a pole dancing lesson or group instruction on tantric sex. Planners, this is not the time to act out *your* particular or peculiar fantasies.
- **Forget emergency protocols.** If there is alcohol involved, then hire a driver. There should be a mop-up kit on hand in the event of excess-related regurgitation. Pack a first-aid kit in case someone can't manage seven martinis and seven-inch heels.

Finally, the Big Day

Here's what I did: took an early swim at the Hotel Bel-Air (where we held our wedding) for a little mind and body alignment before slipping into hair and makeup for my big day. In other words, plan a relaxing activity to calm last-minute jitters.

- **Beauty from the inside.** Make it the wedding day you've always imagined, but leave room to react positively to surprises. No matter what those surprises might entail, your attitude and flexibility (i.e., your imitation of Grace Kelly, Jackie O, Michelle Obama, Hilary Clinton, Kate Middleton, et al., in similarly stressful situations) will be your guests' lasting memory of the event. Practice your poise and grace in advance, using whatever techniques available.
- **Make your entrance a grand one.** Try to visualize that you are a radiant laser beam of light, projecting to all corners of the room. That will help when everyone stops the chatter and focuses attention on you. Just think: All

the rushing around is over. Take your time as you walk through the room breathing in all your guests.

- **Greet each and every guest.** Visit every table during the reception, like the *superstar* you are, and thank each guest for attending. Your face may hurt from smiling, but keep it up—you're halfway through.
- **Now, the parade of wedding traditions.** You're almost home.
  - As the recipient of a toast, the bride does not lift her glass or take a drink. (The objects of a toast should never appear that they are patting themselves on the back, which is why they do not drink along with the others.) The bride instead will listen and smile attentively, and express a gracious thank you.
  - The first dance always belongs to the bride and groom alone.
  - The bride customarily is claimed next by her father.
  - Cutting the cake should be a gentle and sweet affair. By that, I mean, please refrain from shoving cake into your spouse's face.
- **It's like an awards show, so give appropriate shout-outs.**
  - Thank-you gifts for the entire cast—from the bridesmaids to the wedding coordinator, dressmaker, photographer, even your spouse.
  - Handwritten thank-you notes, within a month, for all gifts received, as well as to those who have performed extra acts of kindness—do mention the gift/act specifically.

Runaway Brides, Runaway Grooms, and Broken Engagements

It's one thing to graciously rise above your private embarrassments. It's quite another to weather an extremely public social disaster. Broken engagements are often met with shock and disbelief (and headlines). But as any adult knows, one can never fully understand what goes on between couples. Bitterness spirals out of control, friends will take sides, and brave faces will be worn like masks, however transparent. Checklist:

- **Be civil.** Choose a confidant, one known for trust and discretion. Apart from that, refrain from bad-mouthing your former partner. This is a small town. Okay, every town is a small town.
- **Know the rules.** Traditional etiquette dictates that the lady always returns the engagement ring if it has been her decision to call off the wedding. On the contrary, if her fiancé calls off the wedding for any reason, she is absolutely entitled to keep the ring, toss it in the ocean, or hawk it and buy a shiny red car. Substitute gender pronouns, as necessary. As I wrote at the time of Kim Kardashian's public heartbreak with Kris Humphries, "The wedding ring is seen as a gift from the groom to the bride. Since the wedding did actually take place and the wedding ring was not an heirloom from Kris' family, it is perfectly acceptable for Kim to keep her 16.5-carat emerald ring."
- **Formal announcements.** No formal announcement or explanation is necessary. Such occasions are best kept private. In this case, the bride's mother (or a dear friend) would send brief notes informing guests of the broken engagement.
- **Notify the papers.** If any announcements have been made to the local papers, then whoever originally submitted the announcement should send the correction.
- **Return the gifts.** All wedding presents that have been received previously and/or any monies that have been gifted to the couple must be returned with a handwritten note expressing sincere gratitude.

9

Planes, Trains, Roads, and Rage

Living in Beverly Hills is living in a bubble—a closed, climate-controlled oasis of serenity and order. We are surrounded by the surging, chaotic LA basin that stretches for miles in every direction, stopped only by the mountains and the sea. Around us, millions of people hurrying to work, rushing home, stacked up in bumper-to-bumper traffic. But here? *Sigh*. Peace and quiet. You will, however, be forced to occasionally leave that peace and quiet. You might go in search of antiques at a flea market. Catch a cultural event downtown. See the Dodgers play. Visit an impoverished relative. Whatever it is, Los Angeles is a terrifying place for anyone accustomed to never straying very far away from a security guard. Oh my Lord, you might have to even get on the freeway.

Bonus Tip

Auto entry/egress. Remember the quintessential '80s hit by Missing Persons, "Nobody Walks in LA"? People, we live in our cars. So we'd better discuss the correct ways to enter and exit a motorized vehicle, because I'm certain you're doing it wrong. Wear an undergarment if you're in a skirt, dress, kilt, loose shorts, mini-sari, robe, or nightgown. Many a celeb has inadvertently awarded the paparazzi a magnanimous Christmas bonus when sliding out of a limousine, three sheets to the wind, legs splayed in four directions. I trust that you would rather not open a tabloid newspaper to find a blow-up of your personal anatomy because you decided to go "commando" without reading the following tips. One, always back into a car seat, then pivot and tuck your legs, keeping your knees *glued together* through the entire movement. Two, apply similar knee-lock discipline to your exit, pivoting diagonally and gingerly stepping out; reach for a hand or a handy car part for support if needed.

Bumper-to-Bumper Frustration

I love driving. Put me behind the wheel with some good tunes on the radio (or satellite) and I am one with the road. I am a much better driver than passenger but there is always someone who ruins it for me (and everyone else). Someone who treats Wilshire Boulevard as a mosh pit for automobiles or has their head in the clouds with a lead foot, or believes a yellow light means *make that left turn*, even though that light turned red ten seconds ago.

When another driver exhibits bad behavior, don't let your animal brain convince you it was a personal affront. That man giving you the finger has no idea how much you give to charity. That lady who just cut you off has a car full of kids battling each other. And we know that no one in the world gets a full eight hours of sleep anymore.

Likewise, don't *you* take your frustrations with your spouse, your job, your bills, your kids, or the third season of *Downton Abbey* out on the driving public. If you over-booked, dawdled, or forgot an appointment, don't take it out on your fellow drivers. Don't test the theory that everyone's carrying a gun by pushing road rules past a level of reason, either. Hey, sometimes you will make an innocent mistake and another driver will treat you as though you just brought them the wrong latté—with screams and obscene hand gestures. Who needs it? Rules for the road:

- **Go early, not late.** Those extra minutes staring at yourself in the bathroom mirror are far less enriching than arriving at your destination without a series of near-misses in traffic.
- **Stay off the phone, if you can.** I understand the opportunity, stuck in the car for an hour with nothing to do, nothing to focus on, nothing to—*crash!* I understand you're in demand by very important people. But focusing on a conversation while driving puts you in the same category as someone who's had a couple martinis. Really? Yes.
- **If someone cuts you off or otherwise disses you.** In traffic, train yourself to emit a mantra, such as, "Oh my goodness gracious, driver school for everyone," instead of

a string of epithets spit loudly in a coronary-threatening rage from your beet-red face.

- **Every car comes equipped with a horn to be used in emergencies.** Unfortunately, we hear it not only in emergencies, but also with the frequency that one uses the word "ummmmm" or "like"—with equal inappropriateness. Do not honk if you hate traffic. Everyone hates traffic. You risk giving someone else a coronary. Well, perhaps it's acceptable to honk as a warning, if you're strapped for time and have to run a yellow, or to prevent a major accident.
- **If you have children in the car.** Be extra-extra-extra careful because you need to set a good example, not teach youngsters fresh new profanities to try out on the playground.
- **Never give someone the "finger."** Everyone makes mistakes. You just gave the finger to an actor you love on television. Aren't you the dope now?

Brother, Can You Spare a Parking Space?

What did you do on your trip to LA? friends will ask. If you're truthful, you'll say: "I drove around looking for parking." Because that's how most Angelenos spend their days. Here in Beverly Hills, you just valet your car at a restaurant, regardless of whether you're lunching there or not. It may seem odd to hand the keys to your $95,000 Bentley to a complete stranger. Nevertheless, that's the drill. Meanwhile, here are a few tips that will save your life as you drive around the block a fourth time, praying to the patron saint of parking spaces.

- **Don't steal.** Refrain from stealing a parking space from someone who is clearly waiting for that space. That someone might be the person you're about to meet with to get work (or an acquaintance of your dear friend—*embarrassing*).

- **Loading zones.** If you're running a quick errand, utilize the ten-minute loading zone. Just make it quick and pray there are no meter maids lurking in the nearby bushes.
- **Keep change in the car.** Don't get caught without. Most of the meters now accept credit cards, but if you find yourself caught in an old part of town, you'll need a standby stash just in case. You don't want to miss an important meeting because you're running around trying to break a twenty.
- **Avoid tow-away zones.** The threat is real.
- **Don't abuse a handicapped parking placard.** Yes, you're so *connected* that you can probably obtain a blue parking pass and park in those sweet spots reserved for the disabled. One word: Karma.
- **Save a stranger from a ticket.** The meter is strobing red, a parking cop is approaching, and the owner of the car is nowhere to be seen? Oh, your little act of sparing a quarter to stop someone from getting a $60 ticket will show God and everybody else how awesome you are. Again: Karma.
- **Accept your parking ticket with grace.** Yes, it would be nice if they were kind and reasonable and stopped writing the ticket as you run frantically toward your car, quarter in hand. Don't scream at them for doing their job because you parked in a five-minute loading zone and took ten minutes. Do you think that man or woman writing your ticket aspired to work in parking enforcement? No, he or she wanted to be a famous actor, like everyone else here.
- **Pay your parking ticket on time.** Otherwise responsible people routinely get their cars impounded here for failing to pay multiple tickets.

Bonus Tip

Get on the bus. Although most residents of Beverly Hills would rather spend an afternoon with Donald Trump than be seen riding a bus, the nannies and housekeepers who serve the residents of Beverly Hills regularly ride the bus. However, in any other metropolis across the globe, everyone rides the bus regardless of social status. I expect you to learn good public transportation manners, whether you intend to ever use them or not. Offer your seat to seniors, don't forcibly include everyone on your phone conversation, and skip the snacking unless absolutely starving for immediate nutrients. Don't leave litter on the bus. Don't take the front seats unless you're disabled; they are generally reserved for people who need them.

Civil Aviation

Okay, the skies may be friendly, but getting to those skies has become a nightmare to the well-mannered individual. When I was a child, air travel was something of an occasion, and the entire experience was extremely civilized, start to finish.

Throughout the years, airplane food has become a national punch line, and at some point the airlines just gave up on everything else. Economy class guarantees you are packed in the cabin like extras in a crowded dance club scene, and legroom is at such a premium that most of us feel like we are traveling in a fetal position. The last decade has brought security restrictions (shoe and clothing removal, toiletry disclosure, and TSA pat down anyone?) that make a plane ride more of a humiliating hassle than an adventure.

Accordingly, travelers treat air travel like a necessary inconvenience, or worse. They dress for the beach, for the gym, or for an afternoon nap. They brace themselves for delays, incessant nickel-and-dime airline policies, and exorbitant, taste-free cuisine. In other words, travelers prepare for the least civilized experience possible.

This saddens me because flying through the clouds to new and exotic destinations is inherently fabulous. Anything that gets you out of your tired little loop should be invigorating. Also, you'll come face-to-face with hundreds, if not thousands, of strangers giving you an opportunity to put your best manners on display, and remember—smiles and good etiquette are contagious. By pure chance, you may be seated next to someone you've admired for years or strike up a conversation with a seatmate who is truly interesting. Reminder: People meet their spouses in these settings. So stop complaining.

If you go prepared for fun and excitement, you'll brighten the experience for everyone around you. Don't be the person who ruins someone's travel day and maybe even puts a dent in his or her whole vacation. Before you head to the airport, please meditate on the following topics.

Pack up!

- **Dress with respect.** Years ago, passengers dressed to the nines to take a plane ride. Nowadays, we're treated to a scene of oversized tees, polyester shorts, and tattered flip flops. It's entirely possible to look chic while staying comfortable. Select a closed-toe shoe you can easily slip off in security. Don't forget socks of some sort; barefoot at an airport is less than appealing. Go easy on the perfume. In the sealed cabin, you might asphyxiate a fellow passenger who is sensitive or allergic. Don't forget lip balm and lotion to combat the dehydrating cabin air.

- **Don't overload.** So now that the airlines charge for bags, it's a battle of the carry-ons. If it's so heavy that you can't lift it into the overhead bin, it's a suitcase, not an overnight bag. Pack lighter, check it, or try FedEx-ing your heavy items—especially on the way home when your bag will be bursting at the seams with purchases.
- **Check yourself, not just your bags.** If you are in a bad mood, take a few breaths and calm down. The airport and flying experience is hard enough without the attitude. Present a cheerful face, always be courteous, say "please" and "thank you," and be helpful and accommodating. This will smooth over any hiccups. And there will be hiccups.
- **Fly loaded.** If you have ADD, load up your phone or tablet with games or whatever it is that soothes your savage nature.

The security line:

If you have a severe aversion to waiting in line, get in the car or take a boat. Organize before you leave for the airport so you'll be ready to show your security documents, and know all the rules about luggage and items the TSA frown upon. By now you know what will cause a problem in the security line, so don't hold everyone up because you got pressed for time, were lazy, or whatever.

- **Wear slip-ons.** (Easy!) But not flip-flops (unsanitary!).
- **Skip the jewelry.** It will only trigger a siren.

- **Dress for a pat-down.** You'll have the option to refuse stepping into the giant, scary body-scanning machine if you consider it a risk to your health.

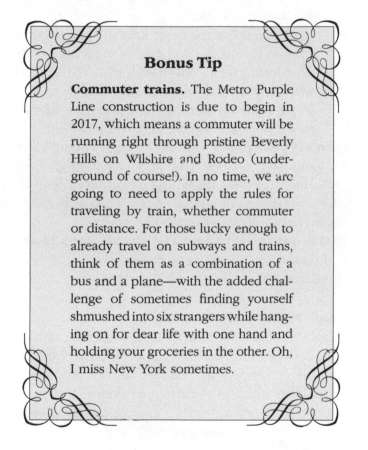

Bonus Tip

Commuter trains. The Metro Purple Line construction is due to begin in 2017, which means a commuter will be running right through pristine Beverly Hills on Wilshire and Rodeo (underground of course!). In no time, we are going to need to apply the rules for traveling by train, whether commuter or distance. For those lucky enough to already travel on subways and trains, think of them as a combination of a bus and a plane—with the added challenge of sometimes finding yourself shmushed into six strangers while hanging on for dear life with one hand and holding your groceries in the other. Oh, I miss New York sometimes.

On the plane:

- **Respect personal space (the lack of it).** In this sealed container traveling 600 miles an hour, everything— chatter, odors, annoying habits—gets exaggerated and

amplified. Respect your seatmate's space and read whatever signals he or she sends. Also:
- Don't bring stinky, messy snacks for the ride.
- If your seatmate is reading, don't start up a convo, you sad, lonely soul.
- Don't hog the armrests; be kind to the poor shmuck stuck in the middle seat and let them have both.
- Be considerate of those sitting in the aisle seats when you need to use the restroom.
- Don't slam the passenger behind you when you recline abruptly. If you can, give a heads up.

- **Turn off your phone.** All the way off. If there's any little, teeny, fractional percent of a chance that a device could interfere with flying equipment, it's better to be safer than sorrier. In any case, don't decide to take that risk on behalf of the 346 other passengers.
- **This is not ancient Egypt and you are not a Pharaoh.** Flight attendants aren't your personal servants. No, no, no, they're not.

Elevator to the Stars

Elevators rides may be short, but they are claustrophobic and necessitate your most thoughtful behavior. Plus, many of them are equipped with hidden surveillance cameras, monitored by watchful security personnel. If you think an elevator is a private space for extra-private grooming, adjustments, or nostril-clearing, think again.

- **Upon entering.** Allow people to exit the elevator first.
- **When the elevator opens.** The person closest to the door evacuates first, unless they are yielding to the elderly, young families, or anyone else in need.
- **Once the doors close.** All conversation should cease or lower to a whisper.

- **Hold the door.** If someone asks you to hold the door, press the open button and use your hand to prevent the doors from closing.
- **Never shout.** Refrain from yelling for someone to hold the elevator or put your arm out to stop the elevator from closing.

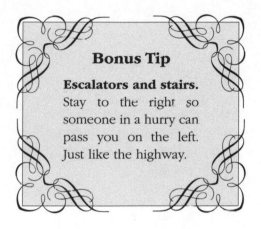

Bonus Tip

Escalators and stairs. Stay to the right so someone in a hurry can pass you on the left. Just like the highway.

10

Child Wrangling

The word "entitlement" gets thrown around a lot these days, mostly on the twenty-four-hour news channels in conjunction with the word "program," specifically social security. I'm here to talk to you about another kind of social security—the illusion of believing one *deserves* good fortune, while not necessarily having *earned* it.

> ***Without entitlement, Beverly Hills would just be a series of stoplights between West Hollywood and Westwood.***

Entitlement keeps the makers of $1,500 Parisian haberdashery and $150,000 Bavarian automobiles in business. You see it every time someone tosses the car keys to a valet without making eye contact. You hear it every time someone sends back a plate of *Osso Bucco* that has apparently failed to aspire to the culinary standards set forth by the best chefs of Milan, whom the diner happens to know personally. The person ripping the poor waiter to shreds over that impossible *Osso Bucco?* A twelve-year-old.

How do you teach *perspective* to a kid whose friends all live in castles and arrive at their exclusive private schools in Range Rovers driven by someone referred to only by his last name? How do you teach values to a kid who will never ride in a pick-up truck unless it's to a *ten-grand-a-week* dude ranch in Aspen, or work scooping ice cream after school unless it's for Mom's yoga-dogs fundraiser?

By the time these privileged souls have graduated from high school, they've logged more hours in five-star restaurants than a Belgian ambassador. They've attended exclusive summer camps and dined on the Riviera (both the one in France and the country club in the Palisades), frolicked backstage at concerts, and cruised on private jets to St. Barts and Tahiti.

A kid's birthday party here can cost more than some colleges.

Everywhere they go, it's VIP treatment all the way, especially at home where the butler, nanny, housekeeper, or tutor attend to every need. I've trained children who were on their way to Swiss finishing schools and been flown to undisclosed locations to conduct private etiquette lessons. So why exactly would these precious little things ever bother to exert themselves when they seem to *deserve* the best without lifting a finger?

Yes, I'm worried we're producing a generation of youngsters unequipped to hear the word *no* without freaking out. If this description doesn't fit your family, it fits a family that your child is carefully observing from a distance via television.

Check Your Bags at the Door

By bags, I mean the baggage from your own childhood, perhaps due to an overly strict home environment or one that was too unstructured. Respect begins at home. Walk the walk. Are you too busy to incorporate good manners into the program? It's not that you're lazy (although some of you are, and others so exhausted that I can hardly blame you). It's that some of us weren't brought up in a polite environment and others are fearful that disciplining their children too stringently will harm the relationship.

Snap out of it! You are not your child's drinking buddy; you are the parent. You do not laugh off your kids' obnoxious antics as you would your college pals. You are in charge. Children, like sheepdogs, thrive on a steady diet of boundaries and discipline. They are also observing your every move for clues as to how to navigate this strange new world. If you don't practice what you preach, you'll lose credibility, *fast*. Minus strong guidance, they will make up their own rules, based on information gleaned from their peers and media.

Yes, they'll find more engaging role models elsewhere, perhaps a violent videogame character or, worse, a celebrity heiress.

Success in this endeavor requires investment, reinforcement, and patience. Repeat the Golden Rule—treat others as you wish to be treated—to yourself, even as you repeat it to your kids. It beats "because I said so" as a mantra. Create family rituals and stick to them. From the "good morning," *every* morning, to the "good night," *every* night, incorporate little anchors of civility into your kids' lives. In other words, start the brainwashing now. Every bit of information that goes into their little noggins is hard-coded (as opposed to the way that info goes into one of your ears and shoots right out the other, like a drive-thru dry cleaner, due mostly to your advancing age, self-preoccupation, and endless distractions). It's time to start studying neuro-linguistic programming and other hypnosis techniques to understand exactly how to get into your youngster's mind on a subconscious level. Think that's wrong? You've never had kids.

> *To teach kindness, courtesy, respect, consideration, and ethical behavior, be kind, courteous, respectful, considerate, and ethical.*

My clear implication, in case you missed it: If you are mean, rude, thoughtless, and a liar, that's what you'll be teaching your children. *Dare them to be polite* (which also happens to be my company's tagline). However, if your brainwashing in the name of good is successful, your subjects will continue to practice their manners even when you're not there. As they fan out into the world, your progeny will recognize opportunities to put their best characteristics and ethical behavior on display. They will look for those opportunities, like little predators of politesse. As adults, they will find themselves consistently acting with honesty, integrity, and tolerance.

Sigh. Job well done.

Fun Is Your Best Teaching Partner

A background in the theatre always helps with children, because laughter is a very effective way of attracting short attention spans while slipping in messages. Props, puppets, paid actors on hiatus from nonexistent television shows . . . whatever it takes. Demonstrate good table manners, for example, by playing the sloppiest of sloppy eaters. Everyone at the table will be horrified, and your kids will take note. Unless your kid is at the age where he or she just discovered what "opposite" means. Whoops, you've just inadvertently taught your kid an easy and reliable way to upset an adult!

Know your kid's triggers and psychological motivations before you start a program of this sort. Also, mocking an undesirable behavior is different than mocking an individual—never humiliate a child for lack of knowledge and please don't teach them to mock others, either. You'll find out why, when they turn it on you. And never turn it off. Here are a few points of entry I've discovered in my years working with children:

- **Explain why manners matter.** If children don't understand the urgency of a matter, they'll wisely ignore it. They have so many more interesting things on their plate—pureed carrots, for one. So eliminate distractions during learning sessions. Quiet room. Television, etc., *off.*
- **Make manners a game.** Kids love games and are (with exceptions) naturally competitive. Create a reward system. As with puppies, you may start with treats and chew toys, but soon they will want to please without thinking about it. Make success *conditional.* It prepares your child for the hard truths they'll face in the future about most relationships.
- **Reverse psychology.** A certain age group will always do exactly what you tell them *not* to do. It's your kid's way of testing boundaries; use it!
- **Trial and error.** Every child uses different skills to absorb information. Some learn by listening, some from observation, and some act it out to incorporate good manners into their daily lives. Figure out which works best for your child and it will become a valuable piece of information to help them in all areas of learning.
- **Keep it simple.** You think your three-year-old is very sophisticated because she can operate a smartphone

better than you can, but her ability to grasp ideas may not be as advanced as you believe. Two words: Tooth Fairy. Talking over kids' heads will bore them; they've just tuned you out, Mom. *Not listening*. Thinking about cookies. Direct, easy-to-understand language is best.

- **One day at a time.** Kids absorb fast, but honing skills takes time. Don't overwhelm them with too much, too soon. Create a calendar for progress and highlight one area at a time—first impressions, introductions, table manners, and communication skills. Set realistic goals for introduction, practice, and mastery (using that term loosely). Never forget these are *children*.

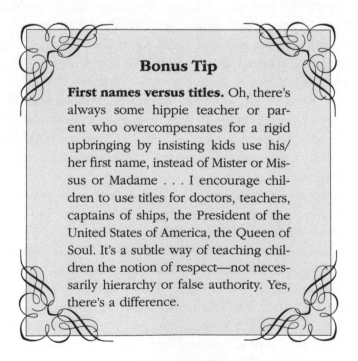

Bonus Tip

First names versus titles. Oh, there's always some hippie teacher or parent who overcompensates for a rigid upbringing by insisting kids use his/her first name, instead of Mister or Missus or Madame . . . I encourage children to use titles for doctors, teachers, captains of ships, the President of the United States of America, the Queen of Soul. It's a subtle way of teaching children the notion of respect—not necessarily hierarchy or false authority. Yes, there's a difference.

Don't Encase Your Kids in Lucite

As parents, we spend a great deal of time banging our heads against the Italian wallpaper, trying to figure out the best course of action for our children. We're trying to give them the skills to evolve into successful, fulfilled (employed) adults. I personally feel that a large part of parenting has a lot to do with prayer and luck. But Beverly Hills is already a refuge of relative safety and comfort. So, it's those overprotective parents who are mistakenly detonating the entitlement bomb. If you completely seal out reality, you're dooming your children to either remain within the borders of the kingdom for the rest of their life—or face a serious shock when they step into the real world.

I understand why parents will do anything to provide their children everything they want while shielding them from hardship (yes, it's sometimes naked resentment against their own unfulfilled desires). But doting and hovering does a child a disservice. I am speaking of the micromanaging, worrying, protecting, and stressing over every fragmentary facet of their lives, plus the endless overscheduling to transform them into little geniuses, added to the relentless chorus of praise that they can do no wrong. All you are accomplishing is turning children into little want-monsters—to be more accurate, little get-monsters.

There is nothing wrong with helping your children develop a thicker skin.

No, I'm not talking about leaving your six-year-old on Sunset Boulevard with a dollar and driving off while shouting, "Home, Lassie, home!" However, encouraging a child to work through difficulty on his or her own builds good character. Encouraging a child to pursue a unique passion with extra effort, that's a gift. Fight the plague of entitlement by taking a step back and allowing your spawn to develop on his or her own terms. Here are my three favorite vaccines against this all-too-common condition:

Grit:

A little adversity is a superb (if not strict) teacher. Of course you want your children to be happy and carefree. But prepare them for discomfort, disappointment, and trauma. Your kids will have a better chance of navigating this merciless jungle (also known as *reality*). If someone does not treat my daughters with respect, they need to be able to stand up for themselves and not always look to me for help. I will have to step in from time to time, parent-to-parent. But I will not always be there to save the day. And no matter how carefully you plan, this day will come.

Resilience:

Success? You can have that with everything going in your favor. *Achievement* is bouncing back from rock-bottom. Hard work can turn problems around. Sometimes, however, it's better to resist conflict and just abandon a sinking ship. Society obsessively equates a "quitter" with a "loser," but focusing energy on fruitless propositions detracts from more productive activities. Resilience means making an exit before things get ugly. Adults, you should also know when to quit. Please apply this to the temptation to get (and stay) involved in useless kerfuffles. My advice, *make a graceful exit*.

Gratitude:

Any tiny, fleeting moment of happiness comes from being grateful for whatever it is you have. Without a pinch of gratitude, those joyful feelings of yours are more likely greed, schadenfreude, or possibly drug induced. Your kids should understand that anything good in their lives did not happen by accident. Make sure they appreciate and thank those who are responsible for their apparent fortune.

> *I've had countless experiences with amazing children who've experienced their fair share of grit, resilience, and gratitude. I've worked with kids on the spectrum with ADD, ADHD, Aspergers, and Autism who've exemplified tenacity and focus soaking up every bit of information I had to share. I've instructed youngsters with missing limbs and those with extra appendages who've exhibited tremendous strength and courage amongst their peers and it has all been incredibly rewarding.*

Bonus Tip

Tackling the tough talk. A grandparent falls ill. The beloved family pet dies. And just about everything you see on televised news is upsetting. Thanks to the programming challenges of the twenty-four-hour channels, we get regular reminders that it's impossible to shield youngsters from every danger. How do you explain the uncertainty of this life without planting lasting fears in your children's psyches? If you are having a meltdown, turn off the news immediately, because it only exacerbates your anxiety. A tragedy of national magnitude actually allows us to focus on empathy. Help your children learn compassion and respect for the families who are experiencing losses firsthand. Teach wisdom and care, not paranoia.

Make the Dinner Table a Demilitarized Zone

We've sacrificed family togetherness in favor of our paychecks, with parents playing multiple roles, all of them demanding. We were promised more leisure time in the future (and flying cars!). Not less. Not *this*. Remember the mid-century snapshot of Dad at the BBQ, and Mom in pearls and a neatly pressed apron in the kitchen, whipping up comfort-starch for the family dinner? How stylish! How nuclear! Now you're lucky if you can schedule a late-night sushi run down South Beverly with the kids between algebra homework and answering emails.

Microwaves have replaced the grill and texting has replaced conversation in many households across America. The Beverly Hills equivalent to this deficit involves sending the housekeeper's son on a California Pizza Kitchen dash. All the while, experts keep prodding us on the importance of the family sit-down meal. Studies have found that it has a more powerful impact than any other family activity. Having regular family dinners lowers the probability of eating disorders in adolescents, promotes better learning, improves communication between parents and siblings, and reduces the risk of adverse behaviors.

And we need all the practice we can get.

I actually received a late-night emergency call one Thanksgiving from a distraught parent who'd just witnessed her sons destroy a hotel buffet. We had to start at page one— how to sit still, use a napkin instead of a sleeve, basic fork and knife stuff. The test was a return to the hotel, for a brunch buffet. I used the dessert table as incentive. It worked, at least temporarily. Practice makes perfect.

*Establish home as a haven of stability—your kids
will be less likely to wander down the
street in search of trouble.*

Oh, the negative sensations associated with the family dinner
table—the over-cooked meat loaf, the heated conflicts, the forced
togetherness, and the straightjacketing rituals. Let's try to erase all
of that and rewrite the story. Begin with one night a week and
expand as needed. Quality time, not quantity. With a bit of luck,
your tribe will soon devour this experience with the same gusto
as they devour an Amy's Organic Three Cheese Pizza.

- **Set up for success.** Express your creativity by recombin-
  ing dishware, glasses, and flatware in fresh, avant-garde
  ways. Pull out your iron and press cloth napkins. Light
  candles. Decapitate flowers. Then stick them in a jar of
  water: centerpiece.
- **Forbid distraction.** Anything electronic that rings, blares,
  or beeps: *off*! God help anyone who knocks on the door.
- **Give the local drive-thru the night off.** Eating can be
  a highly emotional act. Use this point of human weakness
  in your brainwashing strategy. Create a positive psychological association between nutritious food and comfort.
- **Peace through strength.** Encourage (enforce) communication and interaction in a serene setting. No: trash-talking,
  nagging, teasing, cussing, or shouting.
- **A classroom for good table manners.** Let good etiquette ferment and multiply in a consistent, gradual setting until it becomes second nature. Encourage the tribe
  to sit up straight, make intelligent conversation, and conduct themselves with grace and poise. Use "excuse me" to
  leave the table; children should ask permission.
- **Keep it going.** Put away the dishes and pull out some
  board games once a week. Teaching a kid how to play

cards like a shark is a fabulous gift in this burg—because of our proximity to Las Vegas. It's also a nice way for siblings to work out rivalries and resentments in a supervised setting.

Outtake

Personal Space with Siblings

Siblings can find any—*any*—reason to launch a border war. Why not set some ground rules so they can save the fighting for really *meaningful* conflicts? Repeat after me:

- In this house, we ask permission before borrowing an item.
- We are mindful of our siblings' sphere of personal space, about 18 inches in a full circle all around them.
- We refrain from making noise, singing, whistling, etc. when asked to keep quiet.
- We keep our belongings and shared spaces neat and tidy so as not to intrude on or bother others.
- We respect privacy, both online and off. We don't usurp information gathered on siblings' smartphones or try to gain access to their passwords when they are away.
- We never enter rooms or open any door without first knocking and asking express permission.

Outtake

Chores for All Ages

Every little thing you do for your kids, and do without complaint, will rob them of the ability to function on their own in the future when they must share rooms at college, cubicles at work, houses with spouses. Create an age-appropriate menu of chores so that your children will be self-sufficient when they are guests at friends' houses, or at boarding school, or traveling with the circus they've run off to. Kids are perfectly capable of:

- Setting and clearing the table.
- Taking out the garbage.
- Making their bed every morning.
- Keeping the bathroom neat.
- Organizing books and desk area.
- Folding clothes and keeping drawers and closets orderly.
- Turning off lights when exiting a room.
- Recycling.
- Washing dishes and unloading the dishwasher.

Domestiquette

Let's hop in the car and take a drive. Turn north from Santa Monica, on Rodeo or Alpine or Roxbury Drive, to see how the 1 percent lives! After admiring the majestic Spanish and Tudor houses, and their gleaming windows and perfectly clipped shrubberies, you'll begin to notice that the only people on the streets are what some people call domestic help. As they hot-foot it to work from the bus stop, heft a leaf blower, or push a stroller containing one of the little princes or princesses of the kingdom, meet the people who make Beverly Hills an oasis of calm and beauty. Our nanny, Sonia, has been with us for almost nine years. She is my anchor, and a jack-of-all trades. Amongst her main duties as caretaker for my girls, she is also my incredibly inventive handywoman, housecleaner, babysitter, plumber, aquarist, horticulturist, florist, and sous chef. There is literally nothing she can't do, and I couldn't function without her.

I've heard horror stories from friends who've been let down by their nannies in ways I would've thought unimaginable. We are so fortunate. It's crucial to listen to your gut instinct when you hire someone to help with your kids. From the first interview, set parameters and establish mutual respect, trust, and accountability. As I told a group of nannies at the International Nanny Association conference in LA, for harmony to exist and employment to last, both nanny and family must be in alignment and work together. Kids, however, will require some work. They already take you for granted, obviously. Imagine what goes through their soft little malleable minds when they see you snapping orders at the cowering cleaning lady. I would tell you what's going on in my mind when you do that, but good taste prevents me from using such language. Make sure your kids treat anyone who works in your home (or office, or garden) with the same respect they would accord any guest in the home.

- **Your nanny is not your child's personal valet.** She (or today, he) does not exist to wait on everyone hand and foot. Any requests made by children should be done with the utmost respect and in a pleasant, non-demanding tone of voice.
- **Please and thank you are the mantras.** These magic words should be uttered at all times and on a continuous basis. They help to keep daily interactions between nanny and child amicable.
- **Keep conversation good-natured.** It is polite for children to make light conversation and to ask nice questions that gain insight, but do not pry into their nannies' personal lives.
- **Maintain boundaries.** Children should know when they are crossing the line with their nannies on what is appropriate or acceptable behavior. Nannies should not be enlisted to do their homework (except if the parents are out of town, then, of course, they should jump right in),

engage in physical contact (unless they are babies or small children and need to be held, bottle-fed, bathed, etc.), or otherwise be invited into any compromising situations.

- **Show respect and appreciation.** There are small ways in which children can appropriately show affection toward their caregivers. A handmade or handwritten card and small gift given for their nanny's birthday and at holiday time is most appreciated. A friendly greeting upon their arrival, a hug when parting for a period of time, a thank-you note for an act of kindness, and regular use of the magic words go a very long way toward keeping everyone happy and building loyalty.

Socializing Children in the Pack

We've all faced it. At restaurants, theme parks, playgrounds, sports matches. A hapless parent trying to mollify a child careening out of control, like a nuclear power plant engineer furiously (and unsuccessfully) trying to stop a core meltdown. Crossing the street to avoid a gang of seven-year-olds, all armed with matching haircuts some record company stylist forced on a kiddie popstar. Listening to teenaged girls rip their entire social circle to shreds at a restaurant booth, sounding like the Algonquin round table if Dorothy Parker was limited to six words—all of them, "like."

Oh, children. Such an intrusion on peaceful adult society. If you're a parent, think back to the time when you hated your friends for bringing their kids to a party, observing with horror as their spawn gleefully stuck their fingers in the goat cheese and reenacted Pearl Harbor with the crab dip. Parenthood immediately segregates you from everyone you've ever known who hasn't gone forth and multiplied. Must it be so? For every unruly destroyer of appetizer plates, we've also met a perfectly well-socialized child who dazzles us with precocious intelligence and innocent adorability. How do you raise the latter and not the former?

> *One of my most challenging assignments was working with a child actress who wanted formal instruction on how to interact with "normal" people. This girl had spent her young life around adults, most of them either assistants or other celebrities on the set. She had no clue how to engage her peers who were preoccupied by such mundane topics as friends, boys, and sleepovers. I involved her in a series of improvisational role-playing exercises (a language she already knew from acting) to create sample scenarios of just "hanging out"—it gave her the courage to go make new friends, her own age!*

Techno-Babysitting

The sight of a toddler operating an iPad with an intuitive flair you'll never possess is more than a little disturbing: I know. Languages and math and history and art, learned at lightning-fast speeds. But what's your kid soaking up when it comes to socializing with flesh and blood humans? Reading faces for dishonesty? Taking the temperature of the room? Basic human (animal) skills get zero practice.

Worse, that cute little device is also connecting your child to a global jungle filled with digital predators. The TV used to be the babysitter of choice. Now your kids are accessing a world-wide universe of music and games and inappropriate conversations with faceless, anonymous adults. Which means you must monitor everything your kids say and do online. Oh, good, because you already have so much free time! Designate technology-free periods when devices are turned off—certainly at meals and any family gathering. Give kids significant escape from media mayhem.

The Playdating Game

Remember the old days of kids congregating in the neighborhood, riding bikes all over town, hanging out at the local ice cream shop after school? Those days are long gone. For kicks, we used to sneak in to the Fox Studios lot on weekends, inviting ourselves onto the production stages of whatever film or television show was shooting at that time. Not anymore.

The entire infrastructure of a kid's life has changed. Kitchens used to face the street, so Moms could keep watch on the activities. Now kitchens face the backyard, because you'd never allow your child to be exposed to the perils of the front lawn and the terrifying unnamed dangers beyond it. Kids form managed friendships at private school, at temple, at church, at tennis camp, at the club pool—there's no unsupervised playtime anymore, whatsoever. Formal playdates, scheduled way in advance, have replaced those loose, lazy afternoons down at the neighborhood park. Oh, *sigh*.

The Do List:

- Clean and clothe your child appropriately for the event. (This means you, too.)
- Arrive on time. For goodness' sake.
- Offer to bring a snack or pick up lunch. New moms don't get a lot of exercise, so make it a healthy plate.
- If you have an infant or toddler that requires diaper changes or bottle feeding, bring the bag of supplies.
- Don't allow your child to go on a playdate unless the rules of conduct are understood beforehand:

- Use the magic words—*please, thank you*—fluently and often.
- Be helpful.
- Clean up after yourself.
- Be polite and conversational.
- Refrain from any running in the house.
- Don't use outside voices indoors.
- Remind them that even if the host child behaves like a monkey, they should behave like an angel.

- **Sharing is non-negotiable.** If your child is hosting and there are special items they are not willing to share, then they should put them away for safekeeping; everything else is fair game.
- **Arrange pick-up time and stick to it.** Avoid any potential meltdowns at departure. There is no such thing as "just ten more minutes."
- **Tattoo the words "Thank You" on your kid's hand.** As a constant reminder, if needed, to secure an invitation to return in the future, among other things.
- **Exchange all contact info with the hosts.** In case of disaster. Anything from a spat between the kids to a sudden allergic reaction may require your immediate attention. Be reachable.

The Do Not List:

- **Sick?** Don't bring your child to a playdate if coughy, runny, temperature-y.
- **Late?** If you are running late, always phone ahead.
- **No drop-ins.** Don't ask to bring siblings to the playdate arranged for your other children. *Awkward!*
- **Avoid harsh words.** Don't humiliate or severely discipline your child while on a playdate and make everyone uncomfortable and embarrassed. Save your ridiculous outburst for the car ride or the privacy of your own home.

- **There's nothing lower than a gossip.** In this town, that's the worst of all bad reputations. Wow. Mum's the word. Nothing.
- **Don't incessantly brag.** About your kid, about anything. All of us think our own children are amazing. *Oh God, here she comes, with her precious holy child* . . .

Hell Is Other People's Children

Yes, you know that kids are incredibly impressionable. They learn by example—especially by bad examples. All it takes for your well-behaved kid is one encounter with a bad egg, and suddenly the pervasive odor of sulfur and rot has followed you home. Yes, we all parent differently. You can't monitor your child's social choices at school, but you can control your child's social schedule. Group situations might get problematic; although, as is the case with bullying, there's more awareness and policing these days.

As parents, we've all had our share of experience with other people's unruly offspring. Here's the problem: You can't discipline someone else's kid. If we're lucky, we can steer clear of them. But what can you do when the offending children are your own family members or the children of your closest friends?

- **Benefit of the doubt.** Let's start by saying that everyone can have a bad day. You might unwittingly add to it by letting loose on a parent or kid who appears to be stepping out of line. We all do it—misinterpret, misunderstand, and make missteps—from time to time. Take the high road before you get on your high horse.
- **Lightly discipline on playdates.** If the behavior isn't heinous, then a light reminder of certain rules is perfectly acceptable. You can give new play partners a list of your expectations at the outset. If he or she refuses to respect

those expectations, use the three-strikes rule—after the third infraction, that child is *banned*. If you're in a public space, after the third infraction, *split*.

- **Know when to speak up.** There's a difference between unruly and abusive, and that's your action trigger. Your child should never be forced to tolerate abusive behavior at school or in social situations. School officials need to be alerted immediately. If the problem happens in a group, then a short-term solution is needed with long-term follow-up. If you can separate your child from the abuser, fine. If not, then it's time to involve his or her parents to mediate.

- **Involving parents.** Schedule a sit-down with the parents of the abusive child. Meet with an open mind, but remember that apples rarely fall far from the tree and it may not entirely be the child's fault. Some parents think their child can do no wrong (see above). Furthermore, here in this town, it's the unfortunate fact that you will likely have a professional conflict of interest with the abuser's parents. How you navigate this sticky wicket will depend on how much that interest pays. Yes, we all have our price in this town.

Outtake

Petiquette

What I'm about to say will seem inconceivably repellent to anyone who's loved a dog or cat as one would love their own toddler. . . . Okay, yes, I love your precious furry baby, but I love him over *there*, sitting quietly in the corner—not treating my leg as if it were a conquest, or licking the canapés before I've had a chance to taste them, or shrieking at every unfamiliar passerby.

Hey, before I gave birth to tiny humans, I had a tiny Maltese named Max and he was the love of my life. Accordingly, I bought him cashmere sweaters, made his treats from scratch, and threw him birthday parties in the park. The poor thing became very ill and his medical expenses were such that our pet insurance actually dropped us. When we finally lost him, it was so psychologically damaging that our family pets have since been limited to things that live in *fish tanks*. This roster included a blue crayfish named Georgie (an escape artist, he would unexpectedly turn up all over the house!). Now we have a colorful, and rather intelligent (he tells us when he's hungry and mimics movement), painted turtle named Jambalaya.

We often view our animals as people, and we absolutely should. They experience ambitions, victories, slights, affections, fears, and illness, much as we do. In this neck of the world, they often attend parties and power lunches, riding in limousines and staying in the finest hotels. Last week, I saw a Chihuahua in a booth at Nate 'n Al's, noshing on a bagel. And just like humans, animals can be polite or rude, obnoxious or gracious. As you would your first-born, you will train your whiskered friend to be as socialized as possible—for your pet, for you, and for the public.

- **Don't step in it.** You passed potty-training and no longer leave unsanitary souvenirs about the floor, lawn, and curb for others to clean up, right? It's equally impolite to allow your pet to do that, too. Thanks.
- **Formalize introductions.** Dogs and cats don't always appreciate you getting in their face (just like your employees) and they might find too much attention as annoying as you do. Furthermore, like all Angelenos, they'll be suspicious that you want something from them if you're too *nice*. Observe personal space as you would with a human. Always ask and establish boundaries before approaching

a dog or cat you aren't personally acquainted with, especially with children.

- **Invest in professional instruction.** There's more to
obedience training than shouting at a dog to "sit!" Example of common canine crimes: begging, door-dashing,
jumping, sniffing, leash-pulling, biting, and getting exces-
sively territorial. Dogs operate under highly evolved, ritu-
alistic psychological and social norms, and unless you're
an absolute seasoned expert, you still have a few valuable
things to learn (and impart to your four-legged friend).
A well-socialized animal can go anywhere—so you can,
too. Spend the time and money when you first obtain
your new companion, you'll be so glad you did.

- **Travel cheats.** Ever know anyone who has fraudulently
scored a handicap placard so he or she can always nab
the most convenient parking space? Parallel crime: claiming
your pet is a service animal so you two can travel freely. Pet
Partners® is a vital, fantastic service for people with physical and emotional disabilities. It's not terribly *becoming* to
abuse the opportunity, however, just to be able to take your
pooch with you in the first-class cabin. If you do, your
"therapy dog" better behave like a trained professional.

- **Noise annoys.** There's always someone in the neighborhood who keeps their dog (donkey, rooster) outside,
barking at everything that moves, for hours on end, morning, noon, and night. It's an unbelievable way to display
your utter disregard for your neighbors' rights and wel-
fare, as well as the dog. Dogs need exercise and interaction; dogs need a full, consistent schedule of work, dates,
and parties. People need a full, consistent schedule of
sleep. Please, please, please don't be this kind of jerk.

- **Observe pets' presentation.** They say many pets
resemble their owners. You'll never see a disheveled
or unkempt pet in Beverly Hills. Just saunter through

Neiman Marcus on any given Saturday and you'll see an assemblage of pets expertly coiffed, dressed to the nines, smelling like roses in brand-name carriers. These own- ers will have ample supplies on hand, wipes for muddy paws, portable water dishes with filtered water to quench thirst, and resting pads for getting some shut eye.

- **Pet sitting.** Leaving town and need a place to park your pet? Please don't press your family/friends to perform the (unpaid) task of caring for your dog or cat. If they're interested in the work, they'll let you know, and you will compensate them handsomely; trading with a neighbor is also a great option. Otherwise, don't sell a kennel or other professional service short there are a lot of wonderful places where your pets can learn new tricks and socialize with large groups. Collect multiple recommendations for 100 percent trust. Also, find out well in advance which vaccines are required to avoid last-minute hysteria.

- **Love me, love my pet.** You and your canine may be attached at the hip, but that does not give you *the green light*. Never assume an invitation includes your pet unless specified. Untrained pets often leave a wake of destruc- tion, staining and ripping rugs and upholstery! Many of us are allergic. Just because the host has a dog does not mean you should bring your dog—always check to make sure the host dog is good with other dogs. And unless your dog is completely comfortable around children, a pleasant afternoon might end up in tears, stitches, and a lawsuit. Last, better to pay for a dog-sitter than leave your dog in a car for one minute on a sunny day.

This Is an Ad for Summer Camp

I finally joined the legion of parents who kiss their kids goodbye and send them off to camp in the summer. It was like the first day of kindergarten all over again: the excitement of having my life back, along with the sadness of separation. As a youngster, I was shipped off to the Poconos for the entire summer. Back east, this was normal. I gained fond memories and made lasting friendships at camp. So let me write a quick little advertisement on the wisdom of sending your kids off to the woods. Here are a few selling points:

- **Growth.** Camp provides good, old-fashioned human communication and self-soothing skills. Kids have to stick to a schedule, keep their belongings neat and organized, follow rules, and participate in activities. In the age of concierge parenting, kids expect us to wait on them, hand and foot. At camp, they're on their own, sink or swim. Okay, I didn't literally mean, "sink." Forget I used that word.
- **Discovery.** It is a nurturing environment that encourages kids to test limits, find new strengths and skills (archery, basket-weaving!), break out of their comfort zones, and take a few (supervised) risks.
- **Camaraderie.** The social bonds will turn into social skills, well into the school year. Friendships are renewed every summer. There's no tolerance for gossip, slander, or bullying. It's an ideal environment for practicing good group etiquette, in a twenty-four-seven, no-escape way.
- **Getting into nature.** Taking a group hike in the heat of the day, learning how to cop a squat and relieve yourself in the woods, dealing with spiders, bees, snakes, and Poison Ivy, all help children grasp the idea that life is full of discomfort and you just have to make the best of it.
- **Vacation from technology.** No TV, no phones, no iPads. If nothing else, your children's eyes will get a break from staring at a tiny screen and from the relentless stimulation. And no homework, opening their minds to more creative thoughts.

Bonus Tip

Sleepovers. Make sure your child is comfortable and on target with manners before accepting overnights: can keep belongings neat and tidy, check; will offer to help clear the table, check; possesses the ability to make pleasant, respectful conversation with parents, check; and remembers to make the bed in the morning. Good to go? Pack an overnight bag with all the essentials, including cash in case the host family takes an excursion, and arrive on time. Sit junior down the next day to write a thank-you note to ensure future invitations.

Outtake

Birthday Parties for Beginners

You stopped counting many years ago, with good reason, but your progeny regard a birthday as a high holy day. This is an area where classroom size counts against you—all those birthdays, all those presents! How do you keep it fresh? How do you pay for it? When I was a kid, painted clowns and pony rides were a big deal. Can you imagine the level of insanity generated by the spirit of one-upmanship here, in the capital of competitive narcissism? Trust me, whatever you can imagine, it has already been done, topped, stolen, and recontextualized by $500/hour party planning professionals with teams of assistants and a video crew, complete with an Italian director who thinks this is just a stepping stone to getting his arty historical costume drama made.

- **Scheduling.** If you know in advance that your child's birthday falls dangerously close to another child's birthday in the class, think about consulting with the other parent beforehand to avoid overlap—maybe do a joint party!
- **Invites.** Address birthday invitations to individuals or to families, and indicate as such—to "Miss Katie Smith" or to "The Smith Family." Reminder, please don't utilize birthday parties and other such events as a free babysitting service by dropping off siblings along with the invitee!
- **Class rules.** Invite the whole class, a single gender, or five kids or less. More than five kids and word will get out and feelings will be hurt. *Not* hurting people's feelings—that's the six-year-old etiquette watershed—use it!
- **Handling rejection gracefully.** If your child is not invited to a birthday party, then book a competing social excursion with someone outside of that particular social circle. If your little one is taking it really hard, one word—*Disneyland*. (Also, this advice applies to you, the parent, as well. Two words—*retail therapy*.)
- **Prepare for costume changes.** Plan for all contingencies. Toddlers might well spill, so bring an extra set of clothes. Beach to evening? Fill your monogrammed canvas tote and don't forget sunscreen.
- **Appropriate activities.** Choose an activity everyone can enjoy—it's great that you or yours might be champion skateboarders, but those other kids will spend the afternoon breaking their wrists and skinning their knees trying to keep up.
- **The respectful guest.** Remind your kids: It's a privilege to be invited. Smiles, introductions, handshakes,

gifts, gracious thank yous . . . this is the time to put the entire list of good manners into practice.

Children in Tow

As an instructor of children's etiquette, I do my best to follow my own rules as much as humanly possible with my own family. As a mother of two, I also know that traveling with children can be overwhelming, especially with a newborn, with or without the help of a spouse. However, you will want to make your escape from Beverly Hills eventually, whether it's for a quick weekend to visit friends in Palm Springs or across the country to present the young ones to the in-laws in Palm Beach.

Remember, your children are eyeballing you at all times. So be a good role model when you're out in the world. Show kindness and respect to fellow travelers and service personnel. Put your grace and calm on display for them through airline delays, flat tires, bad weather, wretched restaurant choices, crappy service, and unexpected illnesses. How you react to the little vagaries of travel will influence how your kids view travel when they're old enough to plan their own excursions. You'll want them to explore the world, in a responsible fashion, and take care of themselves when they're in uncertain territory.

I hope this list of tips will help make the impossible a little closer to tolerable. Bon voyage!

- **Fun, excitement, travel.** "It's a special adventure, kids. We're going to work as a team to make sure everyone stays together and has a good time on the airplane, in the car, at the rest stop, et cetera. This will not be a vacation from the rules and guidelines we hold dear at home. This is an opportunity to put everything we've learned to practical use, in a really fun way."

- **A little prep goes a long way.** Traveling gracefully takes an enormous amount of creativity and planning. Start by educating the squad about the locale using *show and tell* presentation tools, like maps and travel sites. Pack books, toys, games, drawing pads and pencils—anything the kids love but won't freak out over if the item disappears somewhere on the journey, as I guarantee it will. Make sure everyone gets to bed early the night before departure.

- **Make a safety contract.** Before departure, debrief the pack on all applicable safety tips. Children must not wander, and make sure it's easy for a lost child to contact you. Have them memorize your cell phone number and ask an adult female, preferably, to contact you. Use the "buddy system," keep a headcount, and take this opportunity to enlist kids in a sense of responsibility for themselves and other family members. It's a wonderful little exercise for building self-esteem.

- **Bring fuel for little bodies.** Don't trigger a meltdown due to starvation or thirst (and your deficit in planning skills). Anticipate delays and deprivation, so travel armed with nutritious snacks and water. Don't forget a little gum or chewy candy to protect your kids' ears from changes in cabin pressure as the plane takes off and lands.

- **Accidents will happen.** You will be able to maintain your composure because you will be traveling with an extra set of clothing for each young child, as well as a little first-aid kit and lots and lots of wipes and baggies to clean and disinfect, as needed.

- **Consider taking the train.** Trains offer a relaxing alternative to air travel with kids. You'll still have to supervise them at all times, but this method of travel might be preferable on short hauls. The seating's spacious in the main car, plus, you can get a sleeper room for overnights. Dining cars are perfect for games and other time-eaters. Kids who are nervous about flying won't have the same problem with trains and might enjoy watching the scenery rushing by without the threat of motion sickness.

- **Road trips.** We all remember getting into kick-boxing fights with siblings in the back seat on road trips in the family station wagon. As parents now, we realize how distracting that must have been for *our* parents! It's challenging to keep kids from going stir-crazy and turning on each other, like starving pit bulls, as the hours on the road mount up. Frequent stops and keeping them informed on progress will help quell the oft repeated "are we there yet?" question. Set ground rules before you hit the road with regard to keeping arms and legs to oneself, music choice, car temperature, competitive flatulence, etc.

- **Hotel hints.** Training your child to be a good hotel guest will help in so many future social situations. A hotel stay is not an escape from the orderly lifestyle you expect at home. All rules should stay in place—noise levels, *indoor* voice, pick up after oneself, no electronic devices at the dinner table, no horse play at the pool, etc.

Bonus Tip

Newborn care, on the fly. Most airport ladies' rooms feature a changing table. Wipe the area clean before and after; tightly wrap and deposit that little package into the wastebasket. With nursing, don't get political—find a private place before you whip them out, ladies.

Air Travel with Offspring

Airplanes are uniquely challenging. The confined space means you must be mindful of other passengers at all times.

- Alert the airline in advance, so you can utilize pre-boarding and stroller protocols.
- Avoid "redeye" flights with children who might begin wailing at midnight just as others are finally dozing off to sleep.
- Don't let kids loose, unattended, like baby snakes on a plane.
- Sit between your child and others to act as a buffer between you and neighboring passengers.
- Wait for passengers to deplane before attempting to organize your crew and their belongings—you'll be less likely to leave something behind, and avoid detaining others.

The Holiday Marathon with Kids

The holidays are a family-intensive time, and the relentless, repetitive, agonizing social schedule makes a fertile training ground for kids to practice their skills (and your brainwashing success). It's also the perfect platform to introduce your kids to charitable activities—hit a local soup kitchen together or bake cookies for a fundraiser. In the meantime:

- **Eat, sleep, and be merry.** An empty stomach or a tired little body equals automatic holiday party disaster. Schedules tend to be packed during the season, leaving little or no downtime for children to recharge their child-batteries. Avoid meltdowns by making sure they are rested before arrival and provide a light snack to avoid an all-out assault on the buffet table.

- **Dress for party success.** Keeping holiday outfits clean and pressed will take some planning, but it's key to avoiding last-minute shrieking as you find out that little Oscar has spilled ketchup all over his only decent shirt. Understand the dry cleaner gets backed up at holiday time, just like O'Hare airport.

- **Pre-party briefing.** View each stop as a high-level, high-value event and cover all mission details, parameters, and strategies with your children in the car on the way over. These might include reminding them of names they're expected to remember or the hosting family's offenses that should be ignored.

- **Repeat essential table manners like a drill sergeant:**
    - Wait to be seated until everyone has arrived at the table.
    - Follow the lead of your host or hostess for everything.
    - Place your napkin on your lap.
    - Pass all trays of food to the right and all condiments in pairs.
    - Make pleasant table conversation with the person on your right and your left.
    - Chew with your mouth closed.
    - Wipe your mouth before taking a drink.
    - At the end of the meal, place your utensils on your plate and your napkin loosely on the table.
    - Ask to please be excused.

- **Gifts with grace.** Kids have a hard time holding back when they open a gift and see something they *hate*. Remind them the gifts aren't about *getting stuff*, but the pleasure of knowing that someone cares about you. Drill into their little heads: "Thank you! That's really nice." Like baby robots.

- **Clean getaway.** Have a game plan and a secret code phrase, such as "my tummy hurts," or nondescript word, for instance "tuberose," if necessary to prevent confusion about when to organize a break-out.
- **Thank-you notes.** Start your kid on the thank-you note train early and use every ounce of patience you have to make the experience positive instead of a hostage situation. The repeat gift exchange extravaganza makes good practice. Sit down and write the notes together—go for a win in the cute category and get your kid to write the family's thank you. He or she might feel a swell of esteem from it. Yes!

Sample Thank-You Note:

June 27, 2014

Dear Grandma Betty,

Thank you for the beautiful sweater you sent. I love the color and it fits perfectly. My sister says I should take it on our trip to Switzerland this summer because apparently they have a replica of the Matterhorn in Disneyland, with real snow. Amazing!

I miss you and Grandpa Frank and hope that you will visit us soon. Thank you again.

With love,
Ava

The Bar/Bat Mitzvah Open Season

It's the rite of passage into adulthood for Jewish kids, and P.S., an excuse to throw the most wildly extravagant party you can possibly afford (or charge). You don't know if the kid'll ever get married, so you know—go for it. Invitations arrive by mail in elaborate boxes revealing hand-bound leather or etched glass presentations. RSVPs are addressed directly to the party planner to keep tally. The catering truck? Try a caravan. There will be so many black SUVs parked on the street, you'll think George Clooney's throwing a fundraiser for a presidential candidate.

Come seventh grade, the onslaught of parties will be shocking and awesome, a blur of country clubs and hotel receptions and formal wear in junior sizes. Typically, one well-organized mom will create a master calendar to ensure dates don't overlap. The cost of attending all these formal events will be daunting. Some girls have taken to trading and sharing dresses because there are soooooooo many events. Trying to outdo everyone else is a fool's errand in this town: the more personal the celebration, the more memorable. A hilarious and heartwarming video, well-edited, is worth more than seeing another phoned-in performance by some pop star who owed someone a favor.

If this is your party:

- **Respect the tradition.** Show deference and appreciation to your parents and acknowledge that you're now considered an adult in the Jewish religion.
- **Host graciously.** Make the rounds, and remember all those who have traveled to attend this event. Prepare a short speech to express your gratitude for your family and friends who helped prepare you for this day. It's been years in the making.
- **You'll circulate.** Make your guests feel welcome and engage any guests who are unaccompanied.
- **A thoughtful gift of thanks** to the rabbi, the cantor, and the teacher who have diligently and patiently prepared you over a long period of time is most well-received, as well as a contribution to the temple. Finally, the greatest gift of

all is the one you are giving your parents by embodying a young man or woman of grace, humility, dignity, intelligence, and humor that *is* the bar/bat mitzvah.

Guests:

- **You know the drill.** Attend the religious service, as well as the party, and arrive on time. Don't take snapshots without permission. Turn off your phone and spit out your gum. Adhere to rules and limits. Don't forget to thank your host family for a lovely time.
- **Presents can be simple or elaborate.** Israel bonds, stock certificates, money in increments of eighteen, symbolizing the numerical value of the Hebrew word, "chai"—meaning "life."
- **Appropriate dress.** Classic and elegant with attention to the smallest details. Boys should wear dark-colored suits, a collared shirt, and a conservative tie. Girls should wear a formal skirt suit or dress, knee-length or longer, and if necessary an accompanying wrap, as shoulders should not be exposed in the synagogue. Dress for the ceremony rather than the reception. Cocktail dresses are acceptable for evening parties that don't immediately follow the religious service.

Entrance to Private School Is Destiny

The competition for limited spaces at prestigious institutions is an annual scrimmage, like a bare-fisted pride fight for a parking space at lunchtime on Canon Drive, but with even higher stakes. A great school can launch children on a lifelong path to success; a mediocre school can stunt potential, turn kids off academics, and sometimes land them in a social minefield.

Bonus Tip

Cotillion. Once upon a time, in a less noisy century, young ladies and young gentlemen of a certain prominent stature were schooled in etiquette, social graces, and deportment. Included in this instruction: formal ballroom dancing. For the past five years, I've hosted the "Let's Dance!" Cotillion. In deference to popular culture, I bill it as a combination of *Dancing with the Stars* meets traditional cotillion. I've updated, as required—we don't insist girls wear white gloves (although it is a lovely touch from the past and a practical solution to sweaty palms). Our location at the famed Beverly Wilshire, in the heart of Beverly Hills, is the ideal setting for a six-part crash course in manners and ballroom dancing. Topics include first impressions, smooth introductions, table manners and dining skills, communication tools, social grace, and civil behavior. The dance portion covers the Merengue, Fox Trot, Waltz, Rumba, Tango, Swing—and the Electric Slide! Formal dancing is a perfect way to get young members of the opposite gender in the same room, while developing respect, self-confidence, and proper social and communication skills. It's a far cry from the manner in which kids often get together: In an unsupervised atmosphere where respect gets thrown out the window, self-confidence takes a furious pummeling, and social and communication skills are expressed in monosyllables and creative insults. The last session is a culmination dance party with families and extended relatives present, and it's always a blast.

Private school admission has become a hardcore game of strategy, resources, and iron fortitude, where combatants scheme and exploit any and all leverage. In Beverly Hills, those terms take on a whole new level of crazy. While the city has its own highly regarded public school system, many opt out in favor of private. You'll find yourself cold-calling someone your husband once played tennis with in the eighties who happens to now have a star athlete at your target school.

I've personally tried to avoid this process, but recently found myself right in the trenches with other parents, vying for a spot for my daughter at a coveted school. In every major American city, grooming your youngster into an über-child is par for the course. Parents will call in an army of specialized tutors to teach their kid to quote Socrates in the original Greek. Or pump up a seven-year-old's résumé with tales of exotic travel and experience feeding the homeless.

But these same parents often pay zero attention to educating their children *socially*. These days, children are expected to be as articulate and telegenic as a talk show host. And if you find yourself pleading with a rambunctious child to sit still for five minutes, you'll place a hysterical call to my office. You can't turn a little devil into an angel overnight, and even if you could, would it be enough to fool the school?

You will start training for this prizefight while your youngster is still in pre-school.

Your pre-school teachers will be the go-to personnel for recommendations to your desired elementary school, so start the campaign now. Begin with a general effort to ingratiate yourself with approachable school personnel, volunteering for events and getting a house account at Sprinkles for the monthly cupcake demands. Pre-school is also where the gift-giving tradition hikes up a notch. The offerings will consist of $25 gift cards to Starbucks and other popular local outlets (keep track!) and other minor investments—save the monogrammed key chains from Tiffany's (that comes later). Stick to basics. When living on a teacher's salary in one of the costliest zip codes, anything helps.

Choose wisely. The smart parent elects a first choice and goes all out, using any means necessary, but designates a couple sensible back-ups. It's important to match your kid with the school culture (say, the uptight institution versus the laidback hippie campus) because the best match will produce the best chance in ensuring successful placement at the high school level, which is your actual goal. In any case, your high school–bound teenager will probably know exactly where she/he wants to go. Although, you'll have to decide whether her/his school of choice is a wise one.

Schools say they don't want personal endorsement letters, and yet each morning's mailbag will arrive full of them. Now it's time to work the connections. A glowing letter from someone on the board, or someone loved by millions who went to the school, goes a long way. Your pitch is made at a lovely lunch or dinner outing. If the letter is written and sent, and your kid gets into that school, now it's time to pony up. A gift basket filled with approximately a thousand dollars worth of aged Manchego, fresh white truffles, porcini salt, and Dom Pérignon from the Beverly Hills Cheese Store is not out of order.

> ### *First and foremost, your precious little bundle must absolutely ace the all-important interview.*

He or she needs to be more than civilized, bright, and accomplished—he or she needs to be *likable*. And remember, don't

put off training until the last minute. Start working on awareness of good manners long before the formal interview process begins. At the elementary level, boys are capable of
anything, from expelling intriguing new vulgarities to reliev-
ing themselves in the sandbox. Teenagers can be famously
moody. A trip to the DryBar (a ritzy wash-and-blow salon)
raises spirits. Remind your progeny that everyone is nervous about these kinds of challenges. Some kids have already
become so jaded that bribes are not uncommon.

Oh, and all the following tips to ease pressure on the big
day go for both applicants and parents.

- **Scrub unsocial media.** Generally, this is aimed at high
  school applicants, but increasingly for younger and
  younger people, you need to scan and delete unflattering photos and comments that give schools *the wrong
  impression*. I generally recommend staying off Facebook
  as long as humanly possible.
- **Select a simple, appropriate outfit for the occasion.**
  This is not the time to model any controversial new trends
  in youth fashion; go classic. All pieces should absolutely
  be clean and pressed, shoes polished and free of marinara
  sauce stains. Bear in mind that if this outfit only escapes
  the dry cleaner's plastic wrap for painful formal events,
  your best efforts will probably backfire. A kid's natural
  discomfort in a necktie as tight as a noose will become
  obvious and a distraction. So start conditioning your child
  to respond positively to your selection, like you would a
  puppy-in-training. Repeatedly test-drive the outfit in exciting, fun situations. Make it his or her *lucky* outfit. Then
  plan for a fresh haircut and oversee good hygiene.
- **Arrive ten minutes early.** You've probably already
  driven by the school several times, fantasizing about rub-
  bing elbows with celebrity parents. But you'll need to

anticipate any traffic flow considerations. Don't come screeching in on two wheels and pull your usual predatory parking lot antics. Be nice to everyone, from the guy cutting grass to the lady answering the telephones, because later, they will be adding their two cents to the discussion. Use those extra minutes for some last-minute mental prep (and grooming check). Do refrain from using this time to amplify pre-performance angst. Take the gum out of his mouth. Check her fingernails for traces of glitter nail polish. Or the other way around.

- **Silence all your electronic devices.** Just like at the movies. The last thing you need is you or your kid's personalized ring, handcrafted from a raunchy hip hop classic, to provide some unwanted laughs or inadvertently reveal information regarding your cultural tastes.

- **Enter the room with poise and confidence.** Make a great first impression, standing tall and straight, and initiate solid, sustained eye contact. A genuine smile will effuse relaxed, positive energy. Greet your interviewer using his or her formal name and title until instructed to use first names.

- **Shake hands properly.** It's a sign of deference to wait for your interviewer to extend his or her hand first. If your interviewers are seated, allow them to rise and approach you. When shaking hands, always extend your right hand with a firm grip. If you have cold, clammy hands, rub them together to warm them up somewhere on the way; if they're sweaty, keep a handkerchief at the ready or give a light swipe against your clothing. And don't linger in your nervous desire to connect—a couple of shakes and then release!

- **Avoid foul body language.** Excessive fidgeting and averting eye contact are poker-game signals of weakness. Your interviewer will know you're uncomfortable, would rather be somewhere else, or are possibly stretching the truth. Keep arms, legs, and feet relaxed and uncrossed. Do try to avoid the fetal position even if your stomach is full of barbed wire butterflies and you're certain you've ruined all chances at getting in. You probably haven't. Everyone thinks that. For goodness' sake, relax, so everyone else in the room can relax, too. Smile. Be fun. Have fun.

- **Don't recite a memorized résumé.** Be a good listener. Feel for what's going on in the room. Don't breathlessly interrupt your interviewer in your eagerness to display your vast array of knowledge, skill, and achievement. Instead, just have a pleasant conversation. Also, here's a good moment to remember to do an eye-contact check. Oh, and are you smiling? Smile!

- **Think up some thoughtful questions.** Besides keeping the conversation alive, showing some interest in the school might help convince your interviewer that this isn't a wretched exercise just to please your parents. Ask about the school's philosophy, student culture, et cetera, because your job isn't just to get in the door—it's to decide whether this is the right school for you.

- **Have an exit strategy.** Don't let your interview disintegrate into uncomfortable silence and blatant yawning. Keep your energy up until your interviewer calls time. Remember to shake hands again and thank him/her for the time and consideration. Ask for a business card so you can send a thank-you note. Good work!

You Made It in. Congrats!

Let's get the intimidating truths out of the way first. Your child's circle of friends will have a tremendous impact on your child's self-image, productivity, and achievements—this can be positive, or leave a steaming crater. Each and every new face presents new social pressures for your child. Even at top schools, the staff sometimes spends more time wrestling with behavioral issues than teaching, and bad behavior is the most contagious flavor. You will observe his/her new friends very closely, making a detailed study of the parents and their home environment before you open the social floodgates. A new friend will need to log many hours before earning your trust.

Sample Thank-You Note from the Applicant

January 3, 2014

Ms. Ruth Simon
Director of Admissions
ABC Top School
123 Beautiful Lane
Los Angeles, California 01234

Dear Ms. Simon:

Thank you for taking the time to interview me today. [Name of school] is definitely my first choice. My cousin started last year, and he absolutely loves it. Your beautiful arts wing is the ideal environment to perfect my piano and painting skills. I really liked what you said about my paintings—I hadn't thought about the colors that way, and now I'll think about that every time I start a new canvas.

Thank you very much again!

Sincerely,
Olivia Smith

Sample Thank-You Note from the Parent

January 3, 2014

Ms. Ruth Simon
Director of Admissions
ABC Top School
123 Beautiful Lane
Los Angeles, California 01234

Re: Admissions Interview—Olivia Smith

Dear Ms. Simon:

Thank you for meeting with us this morning to discuss Olivia's admissions application to the [insert name of your desired school]. We thoroughly appreciated the time you spent reviewing the school curriculum and philosophy. The information was very informative and inspiring, and we would be grateful for the opportunity to send Olivia to [the school] in the fall.

We were especially thrilled to learn about your outstanding reputation in the arts. As you know, Olivia is a student of both classical piano and painting. We know she'll thrive in an environment, like yours, that nurtures creative talent. We also value the importance of academics and will strive to keep a balanced schedule to ensure that she works toward a well-rounded education.

Thank you once again for your valuable time and consideration. We will look forward to hearing from you.

Sincerely,
Sandy and Gary Smith

Bonus Tip

March Madness. If you have children here, "March Madness" refers to that stressful month when private schools send out their acceptance/rejection/ waitlist letters. Parents generally care more than do kids—around town, shame and elation and rage rise like heat from asphalt. Mom, Dad: don't get caught up in this silliness. If your child didn't get accepted at your first choice, maybe that school wasn't a good fit. Handle yourself with grace and dignity (if for no other reason than to set a good example for your progeny). Send thoughtful thank-you notes, regardless of outcome. If it's a yes and you plan to accept, send as soon as possible and express your excitement. The same goes if you choose to decline—make it easier on the school, as well as those anxious souls who have been waitlisted. If the verdict is grim, remember that some judgments can be reversed. But don't get crazy. Remember: grace and dignity.

Now let's talk about the specific challenges of throwing your progeny in with the sons and daughters of the outrageous fortune crowd. Some of those kids will be extremely well traveled, and I mean that metaphorically as well as literally. Kids these days have been exposed to images and ideas on the Internet and in video games that would shock even you—jaded, *been there, done that* you.

Carte blanche on three continents? Yawn.

These kids are not just accustomed to being around adults; they're used to giving *orders* to adults. Some of them are even little con artists who have learned to manipulate adults in ways you can't imagine. In other words, parents, you might find yourself outmatched and outwitted by a fast-talking adolescent with a disposable income that approximates your annual salary. So keep your children close and your children's friends closer.

Arm yourself—and your children—with these basic tools and rules.

- **The Golden Rule.** Yes, treat others as you would like to be treated. How is it that this fundamental idea has to be repeated, endlessly, sometimes to no effect?
- **Teach safety as good manners.** Believe it or not, it will make your kids safer. When children are watching out for their fellow classmates (and themselves), they'll be more aware, exhibit better judgment, and fewer accidents will occur.
- **Friends forever.** As each school year begins, the social chaos starts anew. Kids will form fresh alliances and new cliques will take shape. Please convey the value of maintaining ongoing relationships as your kids cultivate shiny new friends.
- **Sell inclusiveness.** Parents and teachers should utilize every opportunity to create an atmosphere in which social leaders include new and shy students, as a matter of habit—not because they're forced to.
- **Say it, don't spray it.** Train your kids to wash their hands and sneeze into their elbows, not their hands. Now go wash *your* hands.

- **Participate at school.** Respect for school administration and staff is non-negotiable. A lot of parents denigrate authority figures in an effort to bond with their kids and show that they are "cool." This strategy won't seem so "cool" ten years from now, when you're bailing your kid out of county jail.
- **Practice good study habits.** Assist your kids in balancing work and play from day one; the earlier they start, the more they'll understand this life is an endless cycle of hard work and not an endless playground.
- **Birthday parties & sleepovers.** Up until a certain age, birthday parties are all or nothing—invite the entire class or make it a tiny, private family affair. Refrain from issuing private invitations for get-togethers like sleepovers at school. Counsel your kids to avoid broadcasting social events that do not include everyone. Then counsel yourself on this little piece of advice.

Zero Tolerance: Cliques, Cattiness, and Bullying

We can no longer claim bullying as a rite of passage. Bullies have become a pervasive problem, and a parent's responsibility in this matter is greater than it has ever been. Kids form cliques and kids get catty, but bullying takes it over the edge. Anyone can be a target—we live in a "new normal" world full of diversity. It's not necessarily being "different" that makes a kid an attractive victim. Bullies are always looking for the weakest prey, the stragglers, the strugglers, those least able to defend themselves.

Kids know that bullying is wrong—in theory. They have attended countless assemblies on the subject and understand that bullying includes physical threats, but other types of abusive behavior live in a grayer area, and it can be difficult to make a child understand that. Children are famous for not comprehending the consequences of their actions. Consider teasing, spreading rumors, gossiping, or excluding someone from the group—these catty, bratty, *unacceptable* behaviors that children engage in regularly can quickly escalate into bullying. Often the ringleader is experiencing some problems at home, and this is where the school needs to intervene.

Technology has created wonderful new weapons for the schoolyard bully.

Once upon a time, the bully's turf was limited to school corridors, playgrounds, and the school bus. Thanks to social networking sites frequented by kids, we've put a new, twenty-four-seven form of ammunition into the hands of bullies. Now bullies have after-hours access to humiliate and harass your child, plus the illusion that they are free to express themselves online because it seems non-confrontational, one-sided, and often anonymous.

Kids post the darndest things, things they'd never, ever say face-to-face (as do adults), believing the consequences are somehow diminished. Also, children rarely operate using the *think before sending* rule. The results can be disastrous, and as a parent, it's crucial you keep tabs on the social battles your child encounters online. Your children must learn that any mean, hurtful, or threatening message, photo, or video they post online is wrong, permanent, and can be used against them and, in some cases, may be considered criminal evidence *in a court of law*.

How does your school deal with bullies?

Every day in this country, thousands upon thousands of kids skip school to avoid bullies. As a parent, you need to investigate how your school works to create a safe environment for its students. When reviewing a school, make sure the staff is not part of the problem, but rather is actively working toward a solution.

See if the curriculum includes character-building and empathy, honesty and respect in everyday learning, as well as tools to make kids feel confident and secure—so they won't need to put others down to feel in control. Make sure kids are getting positive reinforcement that leads to wiser choices and an atmosphere of civility, which outweighs the "reward" a bully gets for negative behavior.

Raise awareness, provide good role models, repeat!

- Have regular, serious conversations with your children about treating others with respect and decency.
- Show your kids firsthand what compassion and kindness and empathy look like (it looks *good*).
- Make children understand that negative role models are often revered in media and exaggerated for entertainment value, like clowns and congressmen.
- We're not hatched with good manners. Regular, repetitive, daily practice is the only way to make these values innate, with room to learn as society innovates and evolves.

Bad Sportsmanship

We've all heard it: "It doesn't matter if you win or lose, it's how you play the game." Well, try explaining that to a movie producer who's taking an autographed hockey stick to a windshield because his life's work just went straight to DVD. And now, try explaining good sportsmanship to his *kid*.

More and more, parents are pushing their children toward high-pressure, adult-level achievement. Mandarin lessons at age five; tennis tournaments at six. It's incredible. Kids have no downtime whatsoever.

Hey, competition isn't evil. It's a test of one's personal strengths. Competition motivates us to expand our skills and achievements. However, in this town, everywhere you look, there is someone wealthier, more successful, prettier or more handsome, leaner, better dressed, more connected, and/or more talented than you.

This town is a super electro-magnet of beauty, wealth, and talent.

It's a town of supermodels, billionaires, and award-winning moviemakers. Success is mundane, it's everywhere, and you can lose perspective, fast. Your little competitive streak will turn this place into your ninth ring of hell, if you let it. And your kids will develop a self-hatred that no child shrink will be able to eradicate. So *let go*. Play fair and play with honesty.

These are the shockingly simple acts that will make you (and your kids) shine.

- **Enjoy the game.** Not the *win*. Make it about practicing skills, enjoying team spirit, and competing against oneself, not others. Downplay the trophy (even as the trophy wife stands on the sidelines, gently applauding, bored out of her mind).
- **Organize grounding traditions.** At home, use family game night as an example to influence your children's attitude toward risk and reward from an early age. Making sure that any organized team sports your kids play include sportsmanship—shaking hands with opposing teammates, et cetera—and will set the tone for everyone to act in a civilized manner.
- **Respect rules.** Take the time to familiarize yourself with the rules before playing, so you and your kids are not screaming at the umpire for no good reason.
- **The ref's word is God.** They have the final word and all team players must adhere to their decision regardless

of whether they agree with it. During games without a ref, it's always a good idea to select a player in advance to make the final call in the event a discrepancy occurs. The last thing your kid needs to see is a fistfight between you and some red-faced, swearing parent who didn't read my book.

- **Everyone is not a winner.** The old maxim of first, second, and third place no longer exists. Team coaches hand out awards for platinum, double-platinum, and triple-platinum so no child is left behind. And we wonder why our children are ill-equipped to deal with failure.

Back to School for Parents

You certainly don't want anyone pointing a finger at your child while saying the apple doesn't fall far from the tree. Infiltrate your new culture slowly. As your child encounters a whole new social set, you, as a parent, will also be exposed to a new set of peers—fellow parents, teachers, and administrators. That means you will be met with new ways to be annoyed, recruited, bored witless, detained from your busy day, asked to do inappropriate favors . . . as well as be pleasantly surprised.

Never forget where you are. Here, almost everyone has an agenda, and admission to this private club means you're a fresh mark. Get ready to be pelted with invitations to ten fundraisers a week. You'll rapidly find out who the jaded housewives/husbands of Beverly Hills are because they're always on the lookout for new partners in crime and misdemeanors. Any professional who thrives on new clients will also mysteriously corner you at some function and give you the business pitch.

If you're a gay parent, expect the same awkward introductions as you would anywhere (probably worse). If you're awkward around gay parents, get to know them personally and see how they refer to each other before you give them any weird labels, like "husband" and "wife." In any case, diversity is a gift and so is imparting that idea to a child. Nowadays, the adults in the picture cover a full spectrum of stripes, and whatever you knew about how babies are made, obtained, or manufactured—forget it. You'll encounter a buffet table of parental situations, so deal with every parent and child on an individual basis.

In Beverly Hills, we face the same challenges parents do everywhere, amplified by about a billion (Euros or Swiss Francs, either will do).

- **Chic cliques.** A tightly knit circle in their Lululemons, draped in Hermés, driving matching Range Rovers. They form fancy side businesses and de-mob to exotic locales together, spa and dinner (as verbs) together. A top tax bracket is the entrance fee to this club. Even if you're in that bracket, think twice about keeping up with these Joneses.
- **The gossip girls.** Not just for girls any more. If you're not nosy, negative, and ready to befriend someone to get valuable dirt, which is then disseminated freely, don't bother applying to this group.
- **Passive aggro.** Jabs, snidery, sucker punches, and cheap shots, all delivered as compliments, the kind you never want to get. Some parents rival hormone-senseless teenagers in their uncontrolled viciousness. *Sorry your daughter didn't make the team. Looks like you're due for an eyebrow wax.* No one is safe.
- **Extremities.** You say Beverly Hills is short on diversity. No, we have extremes, and you'll get whiplash as you're driven to distraction by the super-haute parents with their art collections (name-brand, nineteenth century), bespoke Aston Martins, world-class travel itineraries, and house

staff, alongside the eco-tists, who intimidate with their art collections (vintage folk art and pretentious abstracts), legion of Teslas, holidays in rural Guatemala, and refugees occupying the guest wing.

As a rule, it's always troublemakers who need fresh recruits. Adopt the same protocols you would use at a new place of employment. Greet fellow parents with a friendly smile, but don't get drawn into any negative conversations or drama until you've had a chance to gather as much intel as possible.

The Do List:

* Address parents in a polite manner making good eye contact.
* Include new parents in school activities and special events.
* Establish a relationship with your kids' teachers.
* Make your best effort to donate to class funds, field trips, and other activities in a timely manner.
* Offer to help parents and children in need.
* Keep negative comments about the school or other parents and their children to yourself, the mirror, and your panic room.
* Make the most of your school activities. Go and cheer the team, happily bake the cupcakes, and contribute to fundraisers. Attend school plays and encourage your kids to run for school office.
* Make good study habits part of good manners. Good manners are a matter of self-respect and that means bringing one's best, at all times. You can help by making sure your kids learn good organizational skills and have access to required materials and supplies. And lend a hand to help study for tests and review homework.

The Don't List:

- Judge parents by how much or how little they are able to volunteer at school.
- Attempt to gain favor with your child's teacher by showering them with accolades or ridiculously extravagant gifts.
- Send mass emails to your child's class list unless it's regarding schoolwork or administration issues.
- Hit "reply all" unless the person who initiated the email has expressly requested it.
- Gossip or spread rumors about the school, the parents, or the children.
- Honk, double-park, or block other drivers anywhere near school. Have some patience and take a breath!

Outtake

Parent/Teacher Relationships

- A successful parent/teacher relationship is built on trust and respect.
- It helps to strengthen a child's academic achievements.
- Parents who communicate with teachers exclusively through text and email need to understand the drawbacks of these devices. A negative or angry email sent to a teacher has greater weight in writing. It is much better to discuss delicate matters in person.
- Refrain from copying the administration or head of the school on matters meant for the teacher. Don't be a fink.
- Parents should be helpful without being overbearing and take their cues from the teacher.

Ages and Stages

Babies seem like such unmannered little things, what with the screeching and spontaneous vomiting on people. Here's

> ### Bonus Tip
>
> **Guidelines for teacher gifts.** A thoughtful, handcrafted card from the student is a superb gesture and may accompany a small gift, either store bought or handmade. Gift cards and supplies for the classrooms are always welcome. Sometimes a collection is organized on behalf of the class. In this case, a separate gift is not necessary. Cards and gifts are also a gracious gesture for teacher's aids and specialists if they have regular contact with the student.

a little shocker, though. You can start teaching basic manners around six months. If they hear "please" and "thank you" enough times in the room, they'll learn those words right along with "mama" and "dada." If you can teach a child to use a spoon, you can teach them to use a napkin. Whatever you put in a young mind, stays in. They may seem to forget it, but it's there. Think about it: Teach manners, and those manners will be available to your kids for the rest of their lives.

Here's a handy checklist of teachable manners you can incorporate into your child's life, where appropriate:

From Birth to Age Two

- Learning the concept of *please* and *thank you*.
- Being gentle with animals and other babies.
- Using a spoon.
- Smiling.
- Introduction to sharing and taking turns.

Preschool/Toddlers, Ages Three to Five

- Social pleasantries such as *please* and *thank you, excuse me* and *I'm sorry.*
- Respecting property.
- Treating siblings, parents, and peers with gentleness; not grabbing.
- Learning to listen and observe.
- Play date rules: sharing, playing nicely, taking turns.
- Cleaning up after themselves.
- Not interrupting.
- Waiting for their turn.
- Putting their toys away.
- Covering their mouths to cough or sneeze.
- Washing hands before eating.
- Feeding themselves with a spoon and fork.
- Sitting at the table.
- Asking to be excused.
- Writing their names and drawing pictures on *thank-you* notes.
- Practicing patience and self-control.

Elementary School, Ages Six to Twelve

- Interacting and listening to other adults.
- Proper handshake and maintaining eye contact.
- Making introductions and greeting adults with titles and surnames.
- Obeying rules at school.
- Using correct language and refraining from filler words: like, um, huh, yeah, nah, whatever, etc.
- Writing their own thank-you notes for gifts received and acts of kindness.

- Dining skills—dining out at restaurants; navigating, setting, and clearing the table; utilizing cutlery; handling stemware; making pleasant conversation.
- Good sportsmanship.
- Waiting patiently.
- Refraining from tattling.
- Keeping negative comments to themselves.
- Asking permission before doing something.
- Knocking before entering.
- Suppressing a burp or saying *excuse me.*
- Combing and brushing hair.
- Bathing regularly.
- Sitting quietly for thirty minutes.
- Holding the door open for another person.
- Offering help to adults.
- Answering the phone politely.
- Being tactful and not blurting out.
- Making their beds and picking up after themselves.
- Mastering self-control.
- Observing "The Golden Rule."
- Greeting guests at parties.
- Accepting gifts graciously.

Teens, Ages Thirteen and Up

- Digital responsibility.
- Texting and cell phone manners.
- Emailing guidelines.
- Dating dos and don'ts.
- Interviewing skills.
- Punctuality and time management.
- Sitting up straight at the dinner table.
- Making polite and engaging conversation with adults.
- Taking an interest in culture.

Manners Milestone Chart:

3–5 Preschool	6–12 Elementary	Teens 13 and up
Learning the "Magic Words"	Developing social skills	Using social media responsibly
Concept of sharing	Making introductions	Interviewing skills
Nice touch, not grabbing	Properly shaking hands	Standing for introductions
Putting away toys	Engaging in conversation and small talk	Cell phone etiquette
Introducing patience	Maintaining eye contact	Chivalrous behavior for boys
Not interrupting	Perfecting speaking skills	Ladylike behavior for girls
Waiting their turn	Noticing body language	Texting rules and regulations
Sensing when to listen and observe	Interacting with adults	Emailing etiquette
Smiling	Opening doors for others	Texting guidelines
Saying sorry	Offering a seat to an adult	Impeccable posture and poise
Covering mouth to cough or sneeze	Setting the table	Dressing appropriately for the occasion
Washing hands before eating	Proper napkin usage	Dating dos and don'ts
Sitting at the table	Navigating the table	Making polite and engaging conversation

Using a fork and spoon	Handling cutlery and stemware	First job and developing a work ethic
Putting napkins in laps	Sampling new foods	Grooming techniques
Wiping mouths	Clearing the table	Cultivating personal style
Introducing new foods	Excusing oneself	Perfecting dining skills
Dressing themselves	Answering the home phone	Punctuality
Keeping belongings tidy	Pitching in at home / chores	Being a good friend
Simple socializing with friends	Introduction to social media manners	Time management
Picking up social cues and signals	Apologizing and empathizing	Taking an interest in culture

Bonus Tip

The teenies. Let's take this moment to discuss the perils of turning into a teenager in Beverly Hills and Los Angeles, in general. The peer pressure at this age rivals the most hard-boiled, high-security prison in America—if that prison uniform included Tiffany pearls, a Celine handbag, and the latest subtleties in footwear fashion. The impetus to be the thinnest, prettiest, and popular-est is a nail biting competition. I see girls teeter-tottering across streets in push-up bras and sky high pumps, when they should be dreaming of ponies and young adult literary characters. I guess it's a contest between these girls and their mothers, who I equally witness teeter-tottering across the playground in an age-inappropriate slit skirt and five-inch wedges.

11

The Un-mentionables

Psssst.
Shhhhhush!
Mum's the word.

Those forbidden topics. Those gory, delicious details. Things
we must never say aloud. Instead, we save it for the privacy
of our pool-houses and air-conditioned vehicles.

It's a mystery to me: what gets trumpeted in this society,
and what gets squelched. In today's world, it's perfectly okay
to talk about your sex addiction to millions of strangers on
television, but we get cagey when asked to cough up details
about our executive compensation package.

There is an invisible line between what's acceptable and
what's off-limits, which we observe as though that line were
a four-lane freeway, painted bright red.

And yet, these very unmentionable topics comprise some
of the most ever-present aspects of human life—obstacles and
hiccups and nasty surprises that confront us on a daily basis.

Some of us pretend such unpleasantries do not even exist.

Especially if you walk around with a constant endorphin rush from excess yoga (which I do *not*).

Is it latent superstition, fear that somehow bad luck is contagious? Even in paradise, certain events are inevitable. It happens to everyone, and by "it," I mean life. Bad news travels fast, but no one likes to be the subject of that headline. The sun may be shining this morning, but when the storm clouds pile up, the downpour can shoot holes through your pretty little umbrella.

We don't talk about it because it's too real—the reality is that we've contorted our values in this culture beyond recognition. There's a winner-loser dynamic to everything we do, as though the idea of a win-win scenario was an alien concept.

That dollar in your pocket used to belong to someone else and maybe the parting wasn't amicable. That fabulous new squeeze of yours has left a trail of bitter, broken hearts a mile long, so don't be surprised if you get some cold stares when you hit the town. Half the room at the funeral service is soaking handkerchiefs, while the other is checking real estate websites because the inheritance check just cleared. Everyone's loss is generally someone's gain, and vice versa.

In any case, you will keep that smile plastered on your face, because this is show business and that business must go on. Rain or shine.

Some talk will always be taboo. But, if we don't talk about these devastating little inevitabilities, how will we ever learn how to deal with them?

So let's get everything out on the table now. Toss that umbrella and put on your crash helmet.

The Money-Go-Round

Inequality has become so vulgar as to demand a national discussion. A money bomb exploded in an airburst, decades ago, and they still haven't cleared the wreckage. Here in the bubble of omnipresent affluence, wealth is worn on designer sleeves and baby-smooth faces. There's zero shame in wearing a dress that costs as much as a college tuition, zero irony in parking a brand-new Prius in the circular driveway of a $10 million home with an appointed gift-wrapping room. And zero embarrassment in sporting a head-to-toe surgical makeover that could otherwise finance a small family in rural Ohio for a decade.

> *Remember the old seventies adage:*
> *if you've got it, flaunt it?*

Here's the update. If you don't have "it," you can *buy* a pretty good likeness, enough to fool anyone but a professional.

In all fairness, it's easy to lose your perspective when the trade papers herald multi-million-dollar deals every hour (change millions to *billions* and you have Silicon Valley, which makes this place look like a Bohemian enclave). The fine art of sucking up to celebrities creates a steady stream of freebies, stuffed into swag-bags and sling-shot by brand marketers at anyone standing ten feet from the designated supernova. You heard me—folks who are already loaded get everything for free: beauty products, limited-edition sneakers, cameras, books, music, Prada wardrobes. Eventually, a ride in a Bentley becomes old hat. A $300 bar tab? Business as usual. That Picasso in the hallway? Original.

Rapidly evaporating from your conscience: the struggles of those who work three or four jobs because everyone you know owns three or four houses. Somewhere, in the back of your mind, you know the game is rigged in favor of those who have already won, and against those who never will, but you're busy wondering how much spray-tan to use. Too little? Too much?

Yes, we spend all day talking about money, money, money. In polite society, we never talk about someone's actual money. Of course, that's a difficult distinction to enforce, since every other kind of personal human overshare is on the table, in pornographic detail, streaming from your daily news site.

> *I know you're curious, but it will never be acceptable to ask how much that jacket, that purse, or that house costs.*

Look it up online, if you can't contain your curiosity.

Your relationship with the almighty dollar most likely dates back to your upbringing and how money was respected (or disrespected) in your household. Some of you were taught that hard work and thrift equaled success. Others may have observed the family elders flush money down the hatch like drunken sailors. Either way, it's how you part with your pennies that says who you are today, whether you viciously and resentfully hoard every dime, or generously and appropriately spread it around.

Please don't be:

- **A window dresser.** Bathing in bearer bonds or just trying to keep up a fabulous façade? In this town, you never know. Take a page from the east coast, old-money contingent— don't show, don't tell, don't discuss. No one likes to hear a brag, however humble. Lavish gifts given to those with far less are no gift at all. Don't remind people that the playing field is extremely lumpy and built on a steep hill.

- **A restaurant welcher.** It's easy to split a dinner bill in half, but a nightmare at a table of six or more (especially for waiters) . . . which brings us to celebrations and other happy occasions. Please consider the finances of all invitees before planning a birthday celebration at an expensive restaurant. Once tax and tip and booze figure in, the fair split on a $15 entrée has sailed north of $60. Many guests will try to penny-pinch ("I only ordered a salad, so here's ten dollars"). Another select few will leave early to avoid the inevitable sticker shock around the table. There are those who make it a habit to throw down a twenty, no matter what they ordered. One or two will order the most expensive thing on the menu, knowing the cost will be spread around. And one unlucky individual will end up covering the shortfall—probably your underpaid assistant, and it will take her six months to pay off the credit card bill. Just pick up the tab, birthday boy or girl, or at least pick up the bar and the appetizers. Note: Considering the grocery bill, it's cheaper than throwing a dinner party at home.

- **A "thrifty" leech.** We all have the misfortune of knowing a friend or relative who pleads poverty when the lunch bill comes, but is secretly squirreling away funds in various stock accounts. These individuals often pride themselves in their virtuous frugality, while freeloading with impunity.

- **A chronic haggler.** Our worst offender has money to burn, yet fights over every cent. Each financial transaction becomes a life-or-death contest, as hardworking vendors get nickel-and-dimed to death. It can become a crippling psychosis as the sufferer grows more and more terrified of getting embezzled, ripped off, short changed, pilfered . . . Everyone in the picture—house painter, web designer, staff, even friend or family—are subject to embarrassing scenes and insulting scrutiny. (On the other hand, those who judge clients by apparent wealth and up-charge accordingly are no better.) Pay a fair price, charge a fair price. Life is too short to sweat every penny.

- **A shmuck/deadbeat.** A friend quietly approaches you for a loan—what do you do? Especially as you know this "friend" has already hit up everyone else in your circle. This is why banks exist. If it's unavoidable, at least put the contract in writing and add penalties and interest. And be absolutely prepared to write it off, in full. If it's you who needs the money, please don't let me see you at a fancy restaurant or blow your "payday" on a shiny new suit. You really didn't need it for the job interview, did you? When you scam money from a bank, it's one thing. When a friend helps you out, you need to respect the gesture.

- **A bad family business.** Don't let money fuel family feuds. If you and your sibling still have unresolved issues, the last thing you need to do is add gasoline to the BBQ. Don't buy a property together, loan each other money, or go into business because it will probably end like those kicking fights you had in the back seat of the station wagon, and it's just as childish. Don't hire your cousin, the contractor, to completely redo the house, because when he completely tanks the project, it will poison family holidays for the rest of eternity. Don't hope your uncle gets you that job, because guess what? You'll have to work twice as hard (and face cold sneers from your co-workers).

- **A stage mother.** Whatever your gender. With the popularity of shows like *Shark Tank*, pint-sized entrepreneurs are sprouting everywhere and they are making bank. Teaching your young ones the value of hard work and a healthy attitude toward finances is smart. Teaching your young ones to sacrifice the innocence of childhood to worship at the foot of the God of Greed is another. Also, maybe think twice about answering that open casting call for "the cutest kid ever." Sure, you might pay for college (and everything else you've ever wanted) by the time your tyke turns six, but we've all seen the "Where are they now?" horror shows.

- **A charity pest.** One positive observation I will make about this corner of the world: everyone I know is involved in causes, charities, and other meaningful contributions. Maybe it's all the overnight success. One week you're waiting tables, next week you're starring in a network smash. Lovely people: don't let it get out of hand. Don't be the person who regularly assaults your business and social list for hand-outs, no matter how good the cause. Even heroism gets tiresome.

- **An ungrateful loudmouth.** Did your stock portfolio take a little tumble? Dry cleaners fail to address a stain on your mink frock? Architect miscalculate the square footage on your wine country villa? Stop crying over spilt champagne. And please don't go looking for a sympathetic ear. Your hissy fit over minor inconveniences will sound like boasting to someone with real, awful, tragic, heartbreaking problems that won't go away with a little retail therapy. Got it?

- **When it's okay to splurge.** When your eighty-year-old mother wants to take a nice vacation while she can still walk. When you've had some great news and want to buy a dinner for all of your friends. When you've received a bonus and want to buy a safer, more reliable car. When it's time to get a bigger house. You are aware that you can't take it with you, right? Use your wealth wisely. Another money neurosis involves actually having it, but becoming terrified of spending it. Especially, when you've really earned it! If you've ever been broke, you know what I'm talking about—the fear that never leaves you. Share your good fortune with the people you love. Create unforgettable positive experiences. Have a good time once in a while. That you *do* get to take with you!

Doing the Splits

As are many of my readers, I am a child of divorce. In fact, my parents had married and divorced each other *twice* before I was seven. By the time they officially parted ways, back in seventies Miami, it was messy and drawn out. This was no "conscious uncoupling"—divorce was still a dirty word, whispered in kitchens, screamed in private.

Cut to Beverly Hills, circa *now*. Chart-topping divorce attorneys servicing celeb breakups have honed their craft to a lacquer sheen. A stable of publicists micro-manage the tabloid headlines, as a phalanx of accountants crunch the numbers on the assets. She gets the Tibetan Mastiff and the vintage Porsche 911; he gets the Malibu beach house. There are no schmucks, victims, or deadbeats.

> *Forget the emotional costs. It's payday.*
> *Everyone's a winner!*

As marriage loses its status as a pillar of society, even as same-sex couples are getting in the game, let's not forget this is a story of heartbreak (and massive legal fees).

- **Think about the kids.** *Think*. Then act. This is one of the most difficult conversations you'll ever have with your children. The utmost care and attention should inform the release of this information, because the world already provides too many nasty surprises. Of course they'll think it's their fault. Be truthful, positive, and open (unless it really is your kids' fault, which is *never*). Read up, consult a professional if you have to, but present a united, strategic front. And listen. Involve your kids in decisions about living arrangements, holidays, and traditions; work with what works for them. Maintaining your children's emotional security trumps your desire to use them as a stick to hit your ex with. Always. Also, your child is not your referee, psychiatrist, lawyer, marriage counselor, or snake charmer, so don't "award" them that role.

- **Manage the news cycle.** Parents, friends, close relatives come next, and make sure that conversation is firsthand or via telephone. This is not fodder for the texting mill. No one who cares should get the memo secondhand. This advice also applies to those who love to spread bad news. Everyone likes gossip, but no one likes *a* gossip. Repeat after me, people: *it's none of my business.* (That's one of the top ten mantras you should repeat to yourself every morning anyway.)

- **Don't alert the press.** The less said in public, the better. Privacy is platinum in this unhappy transaction. I would hope you haven't shared your status with the statisticians at Facebook, but that's the last place a divorce should play out. And, that goes double for Twitter. Don't make your sad story a headline, and the press will move on to something more thrillingly salacious.

- **Dispose of your trash in secret.** Even if you practice Zen yoga monkness, you'll be surprised at the lowdown, dirty things you'll do in a relationship power struggle. And believe me, no one wants to see it, especially you. Also, just as bad roommate stories are eventually excruciating, you would be wise to engage a professional ear rather than subject your friends, colleagues, bartenders, and random store clerks to every plot twist of your ongoing drama.

- **Note to friends: keep a lid on it.** There's loyalty, and then there's the ritual unleashing of all the dirt you've held back on your friend's partner during this slow-motion train wreck. One, it doesn't help. Two, if they get back together, he/she will tell him/her everything you said, and you'll be expelled from this social corner like a watermelon seed shot from a water cannon. Three, don't rush to choose sides if you're friends with a couple, because no one knows what's between two people in a relationship—he may have been embezzling from the joint bank account, she may have developed a penchant for her Manhattan Soul Cycle instructor on those "business trips." Four, this is a company town. You can't afford to choose sides. Think of your career, dear.

- **Skip the coronation.** A recent, unsettling trend has spurred event planners to promote divorce parties, complete with divorce dresses, divorce-themed cakes, and request for gifts. It pains me to need to type this "out loud," but in the poor-taste sweepstakes, this is the gold-tiara, slam-dunk epitome of poor taste. I suppose some might feel this improves on the old-fashioned institution, played out in dive bars across the nation, whereupon the new inductee into singlehood knocks back highballs and cries into his or her beer for weeks and months on end. If you want to start a new chapter of your life, skip the fanfare and acknowledge the transition with a few close friends.

- **Dipping back into the dreaded dating pool.** How long should you remain in mourning? Dip, I say, don't *dive.* Your well-meaning friends will try to fix up and steer you toward repulsive online dating services; don't cave if you're not ready. Processing is not just for computers. Also, please don't use your next three girl/boyfriends as arm candy to show the world (specifically, your ex) how so *over it* you are. Try dating *yourself* for a while to review all your bad relationship habits, fears, and resentments. If you were the instigator of the breakup and dying to get out there, please wait a prudent three months before hitting your town's one-night-stand circuit if there are no kids involved. A more deliberate six months to a year if there are. If you think you need to learn to ride *that* bicycle again, I suggest taking a beach vacation on an island, far away. Or, were you already cheating? Hire a publicist and do a lot of charity work with your new public partner to deflect cynicism and bad press.

- **Cautiously introduce the kids.** Here's the wrong way to do it: Your six-year old catches the naked backside of your new "friend" sneaking down the dark hallway for a snack. Initial meetings may go down easier in the light of day, on a fun outing where the emphasis is not "meet your new step-mommy" and instead, "let's all have a lot of fun together." And perhaps not a traditional family activity, with the implication that this new person will replace your ex. Stage a fresh and lively scenario that will facilitate bonding, not irreparable psychological damage. And don't ignore your date because you're terrified your children will hate him/her with the telekinetic power of "The Fury." You want—always—your kids to observe you in healthy relationships, of all kinds, including this kind.

The Inevitable Loss

I consider myself extremely fortunate. I managed to get to mid-life without losing many friends or family members. However, this past year took a turn and I attended two gut-wrenching funerals—the passing of a friend's son and another for a friend's husband. Both were lost way too soon, leaving a void that was absolutely devastating.

This sunny town does its best to hide its dark side, but there are constant casualties.

For every inexplicable suicide, overdose, or tragic accident, however, there are those luminaries lucky enough to see their star on Hollywood Boulevard before making their exit. Each passing touches those fans who grew up seeing those faces in movies and on television or loved the music and put these stars on a pedestal.

Friends, this is part of life's rich pageant. Everyone has to eventually face it. Stunned, frozen, you pray someone will take command, captain the ship, and make it all better. But no one ever knows exactly what to do or say. Doctors, nurses, and funeral home directors witness these scenes on a daily basis, but their professionalism can only get you so far.

This is where tradition comes to the rescue.

The little customs we've adopted to walk you through this terrible event. Flowers, condolence cards, stranger-hugs, memorial services, and giant sunglasses to hide tear stains. This is a time where you will welcome "going through the motions"—because if you stop to think, even for a minute, you'll be paralyzed with grief.

Pay your respects:

- **Find the right words.** All the clichés sound so wretchedly generic. "My deepest condolences." "Thinking of you." Instead, share your warmest (or funniest—unless it's raunchy—unless that's perfect for the family culture) memory of the deceased. If you were not acquainted with the deceased, then focus on your friend's loss: "I know how much you'll miss your dad/your aunt, and I am here as a shoulder to lean on." Close friends require immediate contact; otherwise, cards are mandatory—and so appreciated. Even if the words sound lightweight to you, the message means so much.

- **Turn up the volume on action.** If this is a close friend, skip the card and become a St. Bernard. The survivors will be overwhelmed, too overwhelmed to ask for help. Family has flown in on red-eyes and the house is crowded with grieving people. Offer to board out-of-towners, drop off dinner, take the children on the outing, help chauffeur the seniors, push wheelchairs, change diapers, do the dishes—anything. Distribute hugs freely.

- **Commiserate on Facebook.** The sense of community can lend support, but don't substitute a share, like, or message for a condolence card or personal exchange. Friends will share pictures and stories on the deceased's timeline and on their own; you can share/like depending on the relationship. Be considerate of the fact that some people will receive this news only via Facebook—don't be cryptic or spread rumors. And please, don't be one of those grief junkies who feasts on such events, writing long, sobbing paragraphs bereft of good grammar and correct spelling about someone you barely know.

- **Observe visiting hours.** This is a private tragedy, not a social event; refrain from dropping by. And no one wants to see strangers at a time like this. If you're invited to the house, bring prepared meals, tasteful bouquets, light reading material, vodka, Xanax—anything to aid calm and comfort. Use your good judgment.

- **Keep to tradition at the funeral.** Even if the weather begs for Day-Glo beachwear, a funeral calls for shades of solemn—coal black and charcoal gray. Sign the guest book and leave a brief condolence message. Please avoid text abbreviations and hand-scrawled Emoji. The last thing the family wants to see in this book, five years from now: "thinking of u <3!!!!" Gentlemen, have hankies on hand; ladies, plenty of tissue and wear waterproof mascara. Even if the service is not honoring your own nearest and dearest, this event may unexpectedly dredge up your own life's roster of loss. If you don't own a giant pair of black goggle sunglasses, make the investment if for no other reason than this is LA; you'll amortize the costs in better restaurant tables and favorable attention from store clerks later. And last, this is not an opportunity to scope dates or schmooze for business. Please don't let me catch you working the room. Please.

- **What about the children?** Use common sense—young children won't understand the gravity of the situation and there's a fine line between comic relief and all-out disruption. Your older children will be intimidated by this horrible, incomprehensible event; please take the time to talk out procedures, as well as the entire combo plate of complex emotions. If willing, kids can participate in the ceremony by telling a story or reciting a poem—it's a wonderful way for them to contribute. People with babies already know to park in the rear for quick exits.

- **Don't make it about you.** Silence the inclination to add your own sorrowful stories of grief with those who have just suffered loss. It will never compare to the raw emotions they are feeling at the moment. And, please don't chastise them for not keeping you in the loop on every infinitesimal detail. It is not a personal snub.

- **Go the distance.** Last, don't be a paramedic in your friends' lives, only showing up at emergencies. What's difficult is honoring your friend's suffering after all the flowers have wilted, showing support month after month, especially if your friend seems to be withdrawn by the loss. I'm not suggesting you force them out the door for a wild night on the town. It's the tiny, consistent gestures of support that define meaningful relationships, and that's not always easy in our busy lives. Besides the sudden, obvious shock of losing a loved one, this notion applies to chronic illnesses, divorces, job losses. And when it happens to you, you'll find out who your real friends are. Sorry in advance.

When it's you:

- **Reach out.** Yes, it may be initially impossible to tell people without *losing it*; this is where friends or family should jump in and help spread the word. Accept help graciously; sometimes it will come from the most unexpected places. When you're ready, and even if you're not, make things as easy as you can on your friends and family—your team—because they are suffering with you and for you. It will be difficult and awkward. There will be long pauses and unexpected tears. But your appreciative stance at this time will help everyone muddle through, including yourself.
- **Prepare for the hideous, mind-numbing details.** Your personal nightmare now becomes a logistical one. Announcements need to be placed in papers and trades, obituaries need to be written and funerals need to be planned. Lawyers and accountants will spring into action, and even distant relatives will start counting their chickens. If at all possible, prepare as much as you can with your loved one(s), now, even if the conversation is uncomfortable. Because you really, really, really won't feel like making decisions when *it* happens. Will the service be public or private—religious or not? You've never been to a church or synagogue in your town—now what? Which charities are important to your family? Rely on professional minds when all else fails.

- **The dreaded speech.** If you've been to a memorial service, you've no doubt been astounded at the raw courage of those speakers who manage to rise above what *has to be* the hardest moment of their lives. Standing up in front of possibly hundreds of people and sharing emotional memories without breaking down. This is where tradition steps up—you have no choice. Even if you have no public speaking experience and you're no writer. Just speak from the heart. Luckily, this one's not about you; this is your lost loved one's last, definitive moment. Break the ice with humor, tell some stories, share some private moments. Know that this is a very forgiving room, full of affection and support.

- **Now what?** Attending to thank yous in the aftermath should not be your burden at a time like this. But if you are able to send a note, however, it might be easier than reliving events over the phone. Also, writing is a good form of therapy. There's no set time limit on reaching out. But it will be helpful to you to keep the connections open, because once it's all over, the last thing you need is isolation.

12

When Things Go Horribly, Horribly Wrong

Oh, and they will. You set out with the best of intentions, but Life is guaranteed to throw you a curve ball, unexpectedly pull the rug right out from under you, or deliver a couple below-the-belt punches. Aspire to rising above the fray all you like, but the world can turn on you in an instant, employing dozens, if not thousands, of agents to annoy, kick, and destroy you, ruining a perfect, sunny day. Small town, small planet, filled with people, all bumping into each other, and then starting a shouting match. And behind every obnoxious S.O.B. is a high-priced lawyer. So if you get into an infraction, intrusion, or contusion with said individual, pray you are both represented by the same firm. Let the suits sort it out.

I hope it doesn't come to that. If things get too hot, as they say, get the hell out of the kitchen. And don't come back until you are breathing evenly. Often talking out a situation between family and/or friends only compounds the situation because none of us communicates at our highest level under duress. Words get misconstrued and parties feel injured. Wait until tempers have cooled before attempting reconciliation.

On the other hand, remember that a text is no way to settle a dispute. Very few of us are expert enough at the art of self-expression to solve the world's problems on a smartphone. Minus facial expressions, tone of voice, and body language, it's easy to turn a simple miscommunication into an epic feud.

Unless it's family, there is (less than) zero payback for calling someone out on his or her thoughtless actions. Strangers might mow you down, but don't take it personally. Everyone has a bad day. It's never about you (exception, see family, above). Don't jump down someone's throat for violating your rules of etiquette. When friends let you down, my best advice is to call it *information*, nothing more and nothing less. The potential cost of an altercation is never worth the satisfaction. Do you have to suffer in silence? No. Just don't add to the conflict. Never shout, and never escalate the situation. Just run. Let's proceed.

Agonizing Apologies

In any unfortunate situation whereupon you have offended someone, you only have one chance to apologize, so rehearse your apologies before making them in person. Choosing the right words takes time, and you might want to write them out. But don't email that, and for goodness' sake, don't text it. Insist on meeting. Both parties should be able to read each other's emotions, body language, and gestures to determine if the apology is sincere and is met with genuine forgiveness. Writing a letter is second best—it's easier for some people to put their feelings into words, but a follow-up, in-person conversation is still necessary.

Here are a few notions to consider:

- **Accidents do happen.** People unintentionally hurt each other's feelings, just like five-year-olds on a playground.
- **Take the high road.** Oftentimes, it's easier to apologize even if you didn't do anything wrong. (Just don't do that in a car accident; it may be used as evidence that it was your fault.) Whether this is for bumping someone in a crowded aisle, or accidentally spilling a certain pseudo-secret, the fastest way to move on, regardless of culpability, is to make the apology and make the exit.
- **The non-apology apology.** At one time or another, most of us have been on the receiving end of one of those "non-apology apologies." The patronizing, forced, condescending apology: "I'm sorry, I had no idea you were so sensitive!" Piece of advice: Never say that to someone. Especially your girlfriend.
- **Always right syndrome.** Remember all those times that you've been wrong: Before you realized you were wrong, you were convinced you were *right*.
- **True regret.** If you genuinely were in the wrong, make an admission of true regret and sincerely apologize. Take full responsibility for your behavior, clean up your own mess, and declare your understanding for the other's perspective. A successful outcome will include a plan to avoid future mistakes. You will be, in essence, asking for forgiveness. I hope you get it. I hope we all do.

Embarrassing Moments

The invisible book of etiquette you carry around in your head would remind you that the less you make of a mistake, the less anyone will remember it. A sudden public spill, for example, like doing a full face-plant on stage at the Oscars. So what if you fell on the stairs? *You just struck actor gold.* Hey, it happens. Gracefully pick yourself up off the pavement, knowingly smile, and shrug to all witnesses. At least you had a chance to entertain an audience and that's all any-one strives for here. You just hope that moment won't find later release on YouTube.

Or how about getting your credit card denied in a crowded Whole Foods checkout line? I saw that happen to a well-known actor, who was extremely graceful about it, knowing everyone in line knew who she was. Anyone who has ever been the least bit broke knows the cold, sick sensa-tion that hits your stomach when that happens. Even if you know the card is good. You could scream at the cashier and imply that a serious mistake has been made. But when the poor thing runs the card through again and you are found out to have surpassed your credit limit, you will be ten times sorrier than if you had just handed her another card and apologized. Especially when she says, "I've been told to con-fiscate your card. Sorrrrrrry."

Grin and bear it. Your monkey brain thinks that if you're smiling, things are going really well. So if you find yourself up a creek, so to speak, trapped in a miserable moment with no escape, turn and grin like chimp. It'll send a signal to your brain to chill. It's quite amazing, how easy it is to trick the brain. Once you've calmed down, you might try a real one. A genuine smile goes much further than showing your fangs and growling.

The ability to laugh at yourself goes to the heart of good manners. Repeat to yourself, *nothing really matters, espe-cially me*. Now that's a security blanket.

Grace under Fire

Flat tire on the freeway? Surprise encounter with an ex and this week's *Top Model*, who looks like you did fifteen years ago? Even if you want to go supernova, you should not. Here, where most people think VIP is an honorary college degree they've been awarded, sometimes they do go supernova, with spectacular special effects.

We're always putting out fires, many of which we actually started. The industry is based on relationships, since most people don't really do anything for those whopping pay-checks. Everyone knows each other, and everyone's watch-ing each other, which means no one has the luxury of a public tantrum. Because we both know, the only return on that investment will be your story on the gossip version of the news at eleven. Yes, it's that kind of town. Just like yours.

Now you know why the Self-Realization Center on Sun-set and countless yoga/meditation classes on every corner of this town are filled with desperate souls who will chant for hours to keep from losing it. Pharmaceuticals arrive in eight-een-wheelers, and everyone is on some kind of a cleanse. The waiting rooms of deep-tissue masseuses, ear-candlers, cranial sacral specialists, Reikists, psychics, acupuncturists, hippie chiropractors, and medical intuitives are always filled. People will do anything to get an edge on their . . . edge.

That's when we look to the book of etiquette, however, because it, unlike certain individuals, will never let us down. What the lower animals call a disaster, a social animal will call a blessing in disguise. That flat tire on the freeway? *Made me miss a meeting on a project that would have been a career-ender.* That surprise encounter with the ex? *Thank God I dumped that sociopath.* A positive outlook will always help you retain your dignity, whatever obstacles come your way. Onward, upward, and so forth, going forth and always in for-ward motion.

In other words, good manners aren't just for show. And here's the dirty secret I've been waiting until the end to share with you.

Good manners aren't for other people. They're about treating yourself with the highest respect.

Oh, you can release some steam later. My advice is to try it in little spurts, rather than let Old Faithful blow. Run around the block, listen to a record you really like. If you're having a bad day, don't get into the car if it's between the hours of 3 and 7 p.m. Because our famous rush hour traffic is the last place you want to get stuck when you're nursing a slow-burning rage.

On that note, let's go out with a bang. Here's my glossary of pet peeves. (Disclaimer: I violate my own rules. There, I said it. I may have been transplanted to Beverly Hills, but I'm a New Yorker at heart!) I hope I've won you over to my side.

Pet Peeves, A-to-Z

A | Aggrandizing. Of the self—It's that giant pat on the back some people give themselves, for every minute achievement. *Bored now.*

B | Bad drivers. Don't be asleep at the wheel and don't play Hot Wheels—focus and pay attention to the road. The point is to get from point A to point B without mishap.

C | Complaint machines. *Everything is always wrong, and the cards are stacked against me, and this world is cruel and unfair.* Welcome to humanity. Or build a rocket.

D | Disrespect. You're at a party enjoying witty repartee with an acquaintance, but when someone higher up on the food chain walks through the door, it's whoosh! *Gone.*

E | Envy. The unfortunate souls who consistently believe the grass is greener for everyone else. Comparison will kill you. Let the fuel drive you to work harder, better, faster, stronger.

F | Fine. My least favorite word in the English dictionary that often feels like you're settling or masking some deep-rooted rage. "I'm fine," snapped in answer to, "How are you?" This actually means, "Don't ask, I'm losing it." If I didn't want the truth, I wouldn't have asked.

G | Gum. Cracked, snapped, chewed, and then drooled. Pop a mint instead.

H | Holier (than thou). Unless you have actual superpowers, or have performed certified miracles by the Vatican, please accept your status as just another face on a crowded planet.

I | Itching. For information, which you will later use against me, or to sell to one of those magazines that we say we only read on vacation.

J | Jekyll and Hyde (as in Dr. and Mr.). They run hot and cold like a faucet that either scalds or freezes you. If I had some warning, I'd be able to put on rubber gloves.

K | Kid gloves. Every conversation we have risks a *Mentos meets Coca Cola* outburst.

L | Line cutting. Let's say we're in line for popcorn at the movies. The previews have already started and, for industry regulars, the previews are vital information, not a way to pass the time. So jump in front of me in line while I take a call *at your own risk*.

M | Mobile cell phone abuse. I don't want to hear your conversation while I'm held captive in the elevator or enjoying a coffee at a quiet cafe. Especially because you think you have to talk louder than on a landline.

N | Negativity. There are those who wake up every morning under a black cloud ever threatening downpour. Don't use me as your umbrella.

O | Out to lunch. Oblivious, not paying attention, or grossly unaware. For example, that cute little French bulldog you bring everywhere might actually annoy people, especially when you let little Pierre leave presents for me on my lawn.

P | Penny-pinchers. Those who plead poverty when the lunch bill comes—next week, you bump into them at the dermatologist's office freshening their filler and Botox.

Q | Quid pro no. He or she only calls you for favors, information, to borrow a screener, to get an introduction with one of your powerful friends. When you need something? *Oh, I'll get back to you next week on that, I'm crazed.* Don't hold your breath.

R | Redecorators. They can't resist walking into your life and telling you in the most condescending way to change your diet, your boyfriend, your job . . . and yes, every time they walk in your house, they start moving furniture around!

S | Space invaders. Six inches from my face is too close as you harangue me about whatever it is you find so pressing. P.S., I'm not listening. I'm counting your pores.

T | Talking while eating. Ick. I found your lunch repulsive before it made its way to your mouth.

U | Umm, like, whatever. You know what I'm talking about? After the age of fourteen, take off these verbal training wheels.

V | Voicemail messages that are aloof and elusive, almost teasing you, and leaving you with the feeling that you must call them back.

W | Worrywarts. When you worry so much about what others think of you that others start thinking that you are obnoxiously self-absorbed.

X | Xcess sighing for effect. The exasperated exhale that adolescents of all ages employ in lieu of the words, "Oh, you just don't get it."

Y | Yes men (and women) who never tell the truth, because the truth is almost always "no."

Z | Zero tolerance. Some individuals live to call out others for even the smallest infraction, whether by accident, misstep, or unintentional guffaw. Relax. Not everyone's out to get you. Just me.

My Final Words

When all else fails, here are the famous Dutch House rules, available on blue and white mugs anywhere in the world. Follow these rules and never get into trouble ever again.

- If you dirty it, clean it.
- If you move it, put it back.
- If you lose it, replace it.
- If you break it, repair it.
- If you borrow something, bring it back.
- If someone needs help, offer it.
- If you do not know, ask.
- If it is not your business, keep it that way.
- If it is your fault, admit it.
- If you want respect, give it.

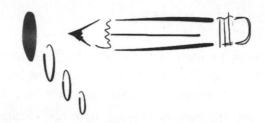

Test Your Etiquette Quotient: How Retentive Are You?

You have now presumably read this entire book, word for word, and I assume you will not look upon this little series of questions as a test, but as an affirmation of your command of etiquette!

1. *You receive an e-invitation to a birthday party, with a published invitation list. Of course, you . . .*

    a) RSVP right away, because you're free that night.

    b) think, *that sounds nice,* and file it in your endless To Not Do list.

    c) scan the list of individuals who have RSVP'd and use a social hierarchy metric to decide whether the event merits your attendance.

    d) you're so fabulous that if you feel like it, you'll show up with your entourage of ten.

Answer: a. Yes, you have three other things you could do that night, but every event equals social opportunities and you are working it.

2. *You're stuck in bumper-to-bumper traffic and notice a driver in an upcoming driveway, waiting to merge into your lane. You make eye contact. He jumps in. You . . .*

   a) flip him off, because letting that car ahead of you could cost you eight precious seconds.

   b) tailgate him for the next two miles, howling obscenities.

   c) keep singing along to that stylish new song they're playing on KCRW.

   d) use this incident as a grand metaphor for your total failure to get ahead in life; kicking yourself, you hit the brakes, make a U-turn, and head for the nearest bar.

Answer: c. Heavy traffic is just one of the many appealing aspects you must surrender to if you live in greater Los Angeles.

3. *A co-worker is quietly feeding defamatory information about the VP of the company (your boss!) to an unsolicited source. You . . .*

   a) dive in and add a bit of your own information.

   b) wave him off with a smile, pretending to be on deadline.

   c) fink on him to your immediate supervisor, behind closed doors.

   d) call him out to demonstrate your loyalty even though you read on *Deadline Hollywood* that half the company's about to get pink slips.

Answer: d. You don't have a golden parachute, so you feign solidarity with the company, while simultaneously massaging your contacts just in case you do have to jump ship. This is called "parallel tracking."

4. *You are at a restaurant, conducting a business lunch. You notice the waiter has added up the bill incorrectly to the tune of $8. Do you...*

   a) gently point out the mistake?

   b) ignore the mistake because there's a half-million dollar deal on the table, and you don't want to look like a penny-pincher, or worse?

   c) indignantly summon the wait staff and possibly the manager to rectify the situation immediately?

   d) step away from the table and discuss it with your server?

Answer: b. Suck it up. It's all of eight bucks.

5. *You've been waiting in a long line at the pharmacy, and it's finally your turn. Your natural inclination is to:*

   a) handle your business as quickly as possible and get out.

   b) complain because there's only one checkout in operation.

   c) take your time; everyone will have to wait like you did.

   d) take this opportunity to ask the cashier if the Dead Sea salts really came from the Dead Sea.

Answer: a. You're already late to your next appointment, so just grab the Epsom salts; they're cheap and effective.

6. *You're out shopping with a friend and she looks like she's been up all night and got dressed in a real hurry. You . . .*

   a) immediately assume her date with that actor went well, and press for gory details.

   b) steer her to the makeup counter and grab some concealer to hide those noticeable marks on her neck.

   c) just happen to mention the name of your fabulous dermatologist because you'll get a 10 percent discount if you bring in new business.

   d) keep your mouth shut and shop.

Answer: a. Anywhere else in America, the answer would be d—you'd wait for her to spill those gory details. In Beverly Hills, what, how long, and with whom is *shoptalk*.

7. *Your ten-year-old came home from a sleepover at a friend's and told you they saw a violent R-rated movie. You proceed to . . .*

   a) mention that you know the girl who did wardrobe on that movie—it's a good time to start teaching your child how to namedrop properly.

   b) call the friend's parents and give them a piece of your mind for exposing your kid to that material.

   c) chastise your child because he or she should know that the rules of your house extend outside of the house.

   d) chastise yourself for not doing due diligence on the friend's home environment and laying whatever ground rules you feel are crucial with the hosts.

Answer: d. Since you've been using your child to worm your way in with this family, who are related to the current head of Sony Pictures, you'll let it go this time.

8. *You blew off a family event to have dinner with a group of friends. The next day, one of them posted a picture on Facebook and tagged you. Of course your brother alerted the entire family and everyone is mad at you. Should you:*

   a) call that friend immediately, screaming?

   b) post an angry complaint . . . on Facebook?

   c) understand that privacy is a quaint notion and realize that you are the bad guy in the story?

   d) resolve to handle it by giving your friend The Silent Treatment?

   Answer: c. Give yourself The Silent Treatment!

9. *You receive an invitation to stay at a friend's home in Aspen. This is fantastic news because you've had a super-stressful month at work. You will . . .*

   a) let someone else take care of you for a week. You deserve to rest.

   b) drink a lot and sleep in and stumble around in your pajamas; man, you really needed this.

   c) rise to the occasion—pitch in, buy groceries, help plan outings, and realize that it's really true what they say: A change is better than a rest. Take a break from doing the dishes and laundry—hey, they have a maid.

   If the answer isn't c, don't expect an invitation from me ever again.

10. *Your new neighbor is regularly throwing parties until late in the dawn hours. Once, you swear you saw an actual elephant peering over the hedges. You decide to . . .*

a) start holding an aerobics class for one each morning at 7 a.m., complete with loud house music.

b) run on over in your LBD that just happened to be under your pajamas and crash the party. Fair game!

c) send over a gift basket with a polite note, asking if they might be more mindful of the noise in the future.

d) call in an anonymous tip to the police.

Answer: b. Obvious. Some might opt for c, or if it's really loud, d. But you never know who you will meet, and life is one giant possibility!

As I drive past the Beverly Hills Hotel, making my way north up Benedict Canyon with the sun shining bright and the wind blowing in my hair, even with all of its craziness and imperfections, I would be hard pressed to find a better place to call home.

Acknowledgments

My deepest appreciation to Diane Diehl, my mentor, who initiated me into the daring world of manners with abounding knowledge and a generous heart, but not without a dash of humor—continuously reminding me to find the lighter side of the material. My husband, Brad, who is my biggest fan and who has stood by me throughout each endeavor from day one. I could not have done this without your constant love and belief in my work. My parents, for their unconditional love. My mother, Linda, who instilled in me the significance of self-expression and awareness. My father, Peter, who introduced me to the importance of detail and the finer things in life. Jill Mazursky, who has taken me under her wing and graciously orchestrated amazing opportunities on my behalf. Lauren Oliver, who has made this book possible by contributing incisive editing, shrewd wisdom, unparalleled wit, and imaginative illustrations. Heather Burgett, who has enthusiastically and amiably managed my public relations and countless other projects with the utmost grace and diplomacy. You are my sounding board. Jennifer Blair, whose relentless coaching has kept me on a steady track to pursue my professional goals. A profound thank you to the committed children, teens, parents and adults whom I have had the privilege of working with over the years and who have confided in me their hopes, their fears, their quandaries, and their quirks. They are a constant source of inspiration and keep me enthusiastic about my work. A special thanks to my sister, Jennifer Caplan, along with faithful family, friends, and colleagues who have supported me from the beginning. Ian Kleinert at Objective Entertainment for introducing me to Skyhorse Publishing. And finally, to Nicole Frail for displaying enormous patience while guiding me through the publishing process; and to Abigail Gehring, Christina Noriega, Bill Wolfsthal, Oleg Lyubner, and everyone else on the Skyhorse team—an earnest thank you to all.

BEVERLY HILLS MANNERS

dare to be polite

Lisa Gaché
Executive Biography

Beverly Hills Manners founder and CEO **Lisa Gaché** is regarded as one of the foremost lifestyle and etiquette experts in the areas of entertainment, lifestyle, and parenting. She provides practical solutions for modern-day living to improve social skills and enhance lives.

Based in Los Angeles, she has become the credible go-to resource for media and the entertainment community, advising on the how-to's of good behavior—from business and interview etiquette to proper dining skills and red carpet manners.

In 2006, Gaché founded Beverly Hills Manners, Inc., an education company dedicated to promoting a *new school style* of etiquette to both individual and corporate clients. Since its inception, Gaché's philosophy has been to teach manners in a way that is both engaging and effective. Her programs and presentations have proven to be a hit with a diverse clientele ranging from the hospitality industry and Fortune 500 companies to academia and the entertainment industry.

She offers a wide range of programs for adults, including her **World Class Customer Service** corporate training.

Gaché has presented her etiquette programming and expertise for a variety of high-profile brands, including **Mattel; Tiffany & Co.; American Girl; Rachel Ashwell Shabby Chic**; **Beverly Wilshire, A Four Seasons Hotel;** the **Montage Hotel** (Beverly Hills); and the **Hotel Bel-Air**, as well as **Oscar**®-winning celebrities.

Often featured on national television (*Anderson Live*, *The Today Show*, *Dr. Phil*) and print media (*Vanity Fair*, *USA Today*, *Los Angeles Times*, *New York Times*, *New York Post*, *Woman's Day*), Gaché is a self-described "work-in-progress" who wrestles daily with her brash New York roots and the casual Los Angeles lifestyle to deliver tips, tools, and guidance for every person in every situation. With gentle humor and a refreshing no-nonsense delivery, she teaches that this is not about achieving perfection, but rather, it's about feeling comfortable in one's own skin and creating an atmosphere of mutual respect.

Gaché received her certification as a *Corporate Etiquette and International Protocol Consultant* from **The Protocol School of Washington** in 2009. The school is the first and only nationally accredited school to meet the high standards set by the **ACCET** and the **US Department of Education**.

Between work engagements, Gaché donates her time providing etiquette instruction to non-profit organizations and local schools for their fundraising efforts. Her experience led to an opportunity to create an eight-week pilot etiquette program for the **Housing Authority of the City of Los Angeles** and an annual program for **HYPE Los Angeles**, providing tools to talented low-income students. She is a host committee member for **P.S. Arts** and has worked with other charities including **Healthy Child, Healthy World,** and **Aviva Family and Children's Services.**

Gaché runs an annual "Let's Dance!" Cotillion Series, designed to meet the modern needs of children by teaching them the social and communication skills necessary to present themselves confidently in an increasingly competitive society.

Gaché shares daily etiquette advice to inspire others to move forward with confidence while being their authentic selves, helping clients refine themselves to better define themselves. While good manners may not always be practiced, they are always in style.

Gaché is a native New Yorker who was raised in Beverly Hills. She graduated from Sarah Lawrence College in New York and currently resides in Beverly Hills with her entertainment attorney husband and two daughters.

Beverly Hills Manners: Golden Rules from the World's Most Glamorous Zip Code is her debut book. Lisa's blog is available on her website.

The free Beverly Hills Manners app can be downloaded for iPhone and Android.

Website: www.beverlyhillsmanners.com

Twitter: @90210manners

Your Own Personal
Etiquette Journal

Here's a place to chart your progress as you navigate life's little difficulties. Don't worry: This is not a test. Use these pages to help develop your own strategies for dealing with bad behavior in your own life (if you're unhappy with friends and family, please remember to make up names!). These pages will help you learn what works and what doesn't.

Keep a running list of your personal pet peeves here (use a separate piece of paper, if necessary!).

Write down the ways in which you yourself often commit these pet peeves.

_____

_____

_____

_____

_____

_____

_____

_____

_____

_____

_____

_____

_____

_____

_____

_____

_____

_____

_____

_____

_____

_____

_____

_____

_____

_____

_____

Record your observations of etiquette crimes in the field here.

Use this page to keep track of unpleasant personal encounters that ended well because you successfully managed the situation.

_____

_____

_____

_____

_____

_____

_____

_____

_____

_____

_____

_____

_____

_____

_____

_____

_____

_____

_____

_____

_____

_____

_____

_____

_____

_____

_____

_____

Use this page to keep track of painful personal encounters that could have been better managed.

_____

_____

_____

_____

_____

_____

_____

_____

_____

_____

_____

_____

_____

_____

_____

_____

_____

_____

_____

_____

_____

_____

_____

_____

_____

_____

_____

_____

**Write down your ideas for handling these situations
in a smarter and more graceful manner, if you had the
chance to do it all over again.**

_____

_____

_____

_____

_____

_____

_____

_____

_____

_____

_____

_____

_____

_____

_____

_____

_____

_____

_____

_____

_____

_____

_____

_____

_____

Congratulations on making it through this intimate exploration and thank you for accompanying me on my expedition through this strange and unruly corner of the world! Please join us at www.beverlyhillsmanners. com to share your stories, thoughts, and grievances. For instant updates, follow me on Twitter @90210manners.